AN INTRODUCTION
TO MUSIC

AN INTRODUCTION
TO MUSIC

Revised Edition

SELECTED READINGS

Edited for the

BROOKLYN COLLEGE MUSIC DEPARTMENT

by

Walter Gerboth, Stoddard Lincoln,
Robert L. Sanders, and Robert Starer

W · W · NORTON & COMPANY INC ·

NEW YORK

Library of Congress Catalog Card No. 68-11199

SBN 393 09790 0

PRINTED IN THE UNITED STATES OF AMERICA

2 3 4 5 6 7 8 9 0

Contents

THE ROMANTIC ERA

THE MODERN ERA

Foreword

These readings were prepared as a part of the *Introduction to music* course, Music 1.3, which is currently taught at Brooklyn College. Together with appropriate listening assignments, these readings are intended to give the student an awareness of styles from the Baroque era to the present. Since neither a prior musical background nor ability to read music is assumed, references to specific works have been kept to a minimum and no musical examples have been included. The readings incorporate general summaries of the styles and selections from original sources.

We wish to thank Frances Steiner Tarlow for her assistance in the preparation of the initial compilation.

Acknowledgments

We are grateful to the following for permission to reprint material owned or controlled by them:

J. M. Dent & Sons, Ltd., and Farrar, Strauss and Co., Inc. for Gluck's Dedication from *Alceste*, as translated by Eric Blom for Alfred Einstein's *Gluck*.

Harvard University Press for "The Composition of Music" from Igor Stravinsky (translated by Arthur Knodel and Ingolf Dahl), *Poetics of Music in the Form of Six Lessons*, Copyright 1947, 1952, by the President and Fellows of Harvard College.

Alfred A. Knopf, Inc. for "Classical Style," copyright, 1956, by David Boyden. Reprinted from *An Introduction to Music* by David Boyden, by permission of Alfred A. Knopf, Inc.

League of Composers Inc. for "The Way of Understanding" by Boris de Schloezer, reprinted by permission of *Modern Music* from Vol. VII, No. 4, April, 1930. Copyright 1930 by the League of Composers Inc.

INTRODUCTION

1

Boris de Schloezer

1 8 8 4 -

THE WAY OF UNDERSTANDING
[1 9 3 0]

A Russian critic and lecturer, Boris de Schloezer has published biographies of Stravinsky and Scriabin and articles on esthetics and twentieth-century music.

"TO UNDERSTAND MUSIC . . ."—this is an expression which all of us, professionals and laymen alike, use constantly, for the most part without considering its precise meaning; without really knowing, even, whether this term "to understand" is applicable to music, whether we can say: "I do not understand Stravinsky," as we say ordinarily: "I do not understand English," or "I do not understand Kant." What difference is there between a musical work which we understand and another which we do not? Is there, in a word, anything which can be understood in a musical work? To understand is an intellectual operation: does music appeal to the intellect? And if we say that it does, if we suppose that the intellect plays a part in hearing music, must we conclude that it determines the pleasure and the emotion which a musical composition affords? Or does comprehension follow rather upon the heels of emotion?

The term "to understand" can only be applied to music if music possesses some meaning. To understand any proposition whatever is to grasp its significance, to apprehend what it

1

means, its objective value symbolized by the words which compose this proposition and the relations between these words. Those who hear a speech can react in different, often contradictory ways to the words of the speaker. From this point of view there is a complete analogy between a mass-meeting, for example, and a concert. Like the playing of the virtuoso, the words of the speaker are the product of certain intellectual and emotional conditions transformed to a series of sonorous vibrations which in turn provoke physiological and psychological reactions in the audience. But in the case of the speaker the reactions are evidently conditioned, in part at least, by the content of his speech, by the meaning of his words. They have a certain objective value of which the words are only symbols and which the audience must understand. If the speaker is urging war and part of his audience understand him to be pleading for peace, we say quite simpiy that they are mistaken, that they have misunderstood the speaker. Language, written or spoken, possesses a content independent of the individual reactions it arouses.

Now is this also true of musical language? Or does what happens in a concert hall reduce itself finally to the psychological condition of the player, to the sound vibrations, and to the multiple psychological reactions in the audience?

It is certain that a melody, a rondo, a sonata are stripped of all rational content; we do not put ideas and theories into music. Theories and ideas may give birth to musical works: but between these works and the psychological, emotional and intellectual soil from which they spring there is absolutely nothing in common. Language is a system of signs which we decipher to get at their meaning, and the whole value of words rests for us in this meaning. But when, on the other hand, we try to decipher the meaning of a piece of music, when we attempt to treat it as a system of signs, to pass through it to something else, we cease to listen to music: we have let the sounds escape and have found nothing in their place. In music the sound system is perceived as such, it possesses for us a certain intrinsic value. It can indeed produce violent emotions and initiate multiple associations, but nevertheless it is as a sonorous system that it persists in consciousness and is enjoyed.

This drives us to the following alternative: either music means nothing, possesses no objective content, and resolves itself entirely into sonorous vibrations that are essentially ephemeral and emotional states: or else the relationship between what we shall call briefly content and form in music is wholly different from any relationship which exists in ordinary language.

II

What, then, is the relationship in ordinary language?

It is one of *transcendence*. The ideas of discourse, the content, the sense of a sentence transcend its form, its sonorous body. To understand spoken or written language is precisely to pass beyond it to get at something else. Insofar as words are only signs, what they mean is something other than themselves. That is why one can summarize a speech or a conversation, extract the ideas and the meaning. Now it is absolutely impossible to summarize a musical work, to extract anything whatsoever from it. If we attempt to epitomize a sonata we simply get another sonata built on the same themes.

It would be a grave error to consider the themes of a symphony, for example, as its content, and to establish in this way an analogy between the development through which a writer guides his ideas and the development which a composer imposes upon his themes. The two fundamental themes of a sonata allegro in no sense "summarize" this sonata; they are not at all ideas in the sense in which we say, for example, that class warfare is the fundamental idea in the speeches of this or that socialist leader. If the musical work possesses a certain content, a significance, if it means something, its meaning is inherent in the work itself and is equally present in the whole and in each of its parts. The content here cannot be external to what we call form: it is *immanent* in this form.

But does this relation of immanence belong exclusively to music?—do we find it also in the other arts? Thus far I have employed a parallel between music and "common language" which is solely a means of communication and quite without esthetic value. But if we penetrate the realm of literature and poetry, we find that the relation of transcendence which binds content and form in ordinary language is superseded by a relation of immanence. The word is no longer merely a sign which we decipher to get at something else that it symbolizes, but now possesses intrinsic value. Although it is easy enough to summarize the average magazine article, summary is not so easy if we have before us a page from some great writer, for his ideas fuse as it were with the words which express them—they are imbedded in, or, rather, embodied in, those words. One may, indeed, give the gist of a funeral oration by Bossuet, but this extract no longer has anything in common with the work of Bossuet. The fusion of sense and form is even more integral in verse. Thus it is as impossible to summarize a sonnet by Baudelaire as a rondo by Mozart. Here we are on the border-line of music, which is the ideal limit (in the mathematical sense of the term) of poetry. Poetry tends towards music insofar as it aspires to immanence, and fails to become music insofar as the words still retain a certain transcendent significance, insofar as we still recognize them as signs.

From this point of view, all artistic activity tends to *transform into immanent values signs having only transcendent significance*. Music is thus the purest of the arts, since it retains nothing whatsoever that is a sign or representation of some other reality outside itself.

4

III

When I read a text, any text whatever, I can interpret it and comment on it in any number of ways but it is impossible for me to extract anything other than its meaning, if it has a precise meaning at all. I read, for example, in the obituary column of a newspaper, that Mr. X has just died after a long illness; unless I read hastily and inaccurately I cannot possibly deduce from this text that Mr. X died suddenly. One conception alone is correct, all others false; since language possesses a transcendent content, this content can be extracted, analyzed, and made to serve as a check upon all other readings. The meaning of a musical phrase (admitting that such a thing exists) is on the contrary immanent in this phrase: it cannot therefore be checked, it cannot be detached and formulated in rational terms.

If we ask a pianist who has just played a ballad by Chopin what it means, the only thing he can do is to play the same ballad over again. But it would be incorrect to conclude that music "means nothing" or that its content is vague. Untranslatable though it may be, the musical sense of the work can be extremely precise, as exact as that of a scientific work. And when I say "musical sense" I am not thinking merely of the emotional repercussions in the audience, repercussions varying to infinity, but of a certain spiritual content which belongs only to this work, which constitutes at once its essence and its form, its concrete reality, its individuality.

Nevertheless the question posed at the beginning still persists. The term "to understand" can be applied to music only if music possesses a definite spiritual content, and this content, if it exists, can only be immanent in the work. But does it exist?

It is impossible to offer a direct proof of this existence, since what this or that work signifies cannot be formulated rationally. But I shall try to show that if we deny all objective significance to the sonorous work, we are driven finally to subjective conceptions that destroy music.

Either the musical work (a sonata by Beethoven, for example) possesses an objective significance, contains a definite spiritual message, like a poem, a novel, or else its text is immaterial only, and there are as many sonatas, opus 101, as there are pianists; or rather, since most pianists do not always play in the same way, as many as there are executions of the work throughout the world. But we must go still further: the execution of the sonata at the concert evidently provokes varied and contradictory reactions among the audience. These reactions, whatever they may be, whoever the auditors may be, are all equally valid. By what standard shall we judge them? What then is a musical work if denied objective significance? A system of sonorous vibrations on the one hand, and, on the other, individual emotions; and, therefore, to go one step further it is a set of black marks on paper, traced by the hand of the composer, which the player deciphers with the help of certain conventions, and which serve to construct sound waves the hearing of which evokes multiple physiological and psychological reactions. The composer of opus 101 is no more, the thoughts, the desires, the images of which the work is the product have vanished. There remain only these marks on paper, a sort of scheme for the player, who is perfectly free to do as he wishes. One will draw out sublimity, another what is merely amusing, a third the grotesque. The player who happens to make us laugh with the sonata, opus 101, will thus be just as right as the other who moves us to tears; only the interpreter who bores us will be wrong. Finally, we can no longer restrict the question to the sonata proper; what is true of it is also true of the interpretation by this or that pianist, on this or that day, in this or that concert hall. There remain then only the thousand varied images in the consciousness of thousands of auditors, images sublime, grotesque, farcical, dull. This is the logical consequence of the subjectivism in vogue with so many people who do not usually think matters through to the end but content themselves with a moderate and comfortable scepticism.

IV

There is still another aspect of the question which it is impossible to neglect. If we consider only the power which music so eminently has to evoke intense reactions among its auditors, and to create among them in this way, for a few moments, a sort of collective soul, a relation then emerges between music and various other stimuli which men have always widely employed. Between the influence of music and that of alcohol, of hashish, etc., we no longer find any qualitative distinction.

Thus today we gather people about a piano and act upon them by means of sound waves; and tomorrow, perhaps, we shall get still better results by means of an electric current acting directly upon the skin. What is important is the result, is it not? All that matters is *what happens* when people are subjected to the influence of these waves, these rays, these emanations.

If music is only the art of combining sounds in a manner agreeable to the ear, in a fashion which gives birth in us to a variety of emotions, I really do not see in what way the art of the perfumer, or of the cook, is inferior. In this case we shall have to admit the possibility of those "symphonies of odors" or of gustatory sensations which the hero of *A Rebours* tried to construct, and shall have to grant them an esthetic value of the same order as that of musical symphonies. A dish, a perfume are as able as a melody to call forth reactions of feeling, images, ideas. There is no reason to stop here: tactile sensations, odors, tastes, can stir up tempests in the soul and produce ecstasies in comparison with which the pleasures of music seem pale indeed.

7

And what is one to do about expression? Has not music a certain power to be found neither in a "symphony of odors" nor in a dinner?

Music is, of course, eminently expressive. The musical work is always the outcome of certain mental attitudes in the artist, conscious or unconscious, whether he wishes it or not; it always carries the mark of his personality, the burden of his feeling, of his hopes, of his spiritual experience. The need for self-realization, for self-expression, certainly plays a very great role in the desire that imperiously drives a musician to creation; and if the labor of creation holds a certain joy, it arises, in part at least, from a very clear feeling of deliverance. But this expressive character which the composer finds in music, depends precisely upon the fact that the musical work possesses a definite content. If the work had no spiritual reality (objective in relation to the emotions of the auditors), if it could be reduced to the numberless mental attitudes which it evokes, it would have by the same token no expressive power.

Now this *is* the case with combinations of olfactory, tactile and gustatory impressions: they are a means of excitation; one may, by using them cleverly, arouse the most diverse emotions; but they have no expressive value. In other words, they offer to the artist no possibility of realizing his personality, of externalizing and of liberating himself. The reason is that they have no intellectual content—"signify" nothing, mean nothing. Art, on the contrary, exists only where there is intellectuality.

If the musical work is not a direct appeal addressed to our intelligence (I take this term for the moment in its broadest sense), if it possesses no objective significance, it can find no place in the domain of art and is indistinguishable from a lover's caress or a cream-puff. This expressive power itself, which we all agree to concede to music, is only the consequence, the secondary effect of the act by which we grasp what it means. We are thus led to the conclusion that the music does possess a spiritual content immanent in the work, which it concerns us to understand.

Still, even those who recognize that a page of music has significance, means something, are apt to regard it not as specific but general and vague, and thus they explain the powerful evocative action of this art, in which each one ultimately finds what he looks for, what he himself contributes, colored by idiosyncrasies of mind, temperament and desire. Metaphysical theories of music—Schopenhauer's among others —consider the matter always, if I am not mistaken, from this point of view: they seek to confer upon the art of sounds a certain spiritual value, a significant content, but hold that this content can only be general and not precise. I myself have upon occasion (speaking of the *Octuor* of Stravinsky) said that music contains no specific idea, not because it contains nothing but because it contains everything.

Now it seems to me that we are on the wrong track here, and that our error is linked with that other fundamental one of confusing the repercussions of music in us—our individual and variable reactions when confronted by a melody—with its significance, its spiritual content. I turn again to the example of the obituary notice in a newspaper. It is read by thousands. Their reactions are evidently very different, varying with the degree of acquaintance with the man now dead. The announcement of this death will be differently colored for each, will carry a burden of varying images and associations. And yet the content of this announcement is *one,* and all the emotions which it can arouse are conditioned by an act of intellection. In the case of the musical work, the content cannot be extracted from the form, the very body of the work; for content in music, as we have pointed out, is immanent in the form.

Everything that floats about a page of music is vague and indefinite; but if it is impossible for us to define, this is not because its significance is too vague and general; on the con-

9

trary, it is because it is *too concrete*. Describing a prelude by Chopin we meet the same difficulty which confronts us when we attempt to define an individual being. The meaning of this prelude is its very aspect. We are dealing with something absolutely unique, and this is the explanation of our impotence in the presence of a musical work, impotence analogous to that which we feel when we seek by formulas, howsoever flexible and subtle, to represent a living being: this Jean, this Pierre, whose very name is a general symbol which does not cover this *hic et nunc*. Only direct contact, intuition itself, can unveil the living being. The musical work also must be seized directly. If the content of music would admit of generalization, a knowledge of it would for that very reason be easy, no matter how fluid and indefinite this content might be.

In the arts where form can to some extent be distinguished from the content (the plastic and poetic), such knowledge is possible, even though it always remains approximate, since the soul of every artistic production is after all fused with its body, as our bodies and souls are fused. The art of sounds alone succeeds in achieving an *absolute* fusion and in creating values, ideas which are concrete beings, personalities whose essence is, so to speak, one with their appearance. From this point of view, therefore, music is the least "modest" of all the arts; she offers herself to us altogether, for she has nothing to hide —her most cherished secret is precisely her surface.

V

Thus it must be admitted that every musical work possesses a certain spiritual content, definite and concrete, immanent, consequently impossible to formulate in rational terms. The emotional influence of the work, its expressive power, depends upon the act by which we grasp its objective content: to be moved by music we must first understand what it means. A

10

reading of Spinoza's *Ethics* can arouse profound emotions in us, but they represent only our individual reactions to the ideas of the treatise, ideas which we must first of all understand, and which are independent of our mental attitudes. The only difference between the work of Spinoza and the sonata, opus 101, is that we examine the content of the *Ethics* apart from the form, while in the case of Beethoven or of any other musician this operation is forbidden. We are thus led to the conclusion that "musical comprehension" presents certain peculiarities; music is not a symbol like written or spoken language but is the very thing itself which it is necessary to understand.

Before analyzing further the sense of the term "to understand" as applied to music, I should like for a moment to consider the sensuous pleasure which music affords, for a good many people regard this as the primordial element of the art, completely independent of intellectual processes. Indeed to many acute minds it seems possible to enjoy music physically, without at all understanding it.

The question then is whether this pleasure is essential, whether it is inherent in all musical perception; in a word whether we are dealing here with a primary or secondary element. Even if it should be established that the hearing of a work is unfailingly accompanied by physical pleasure, it might still be true that this pleasure is caused by something else.

It is necessary, moreover, to rigorously distinguish this sensuous pleasure from the joy, *sui generis,* which every work of art affords, and which contains, esthetically transmuted, the negative, enervating emotions that in real life we seek to avoid: melancholy, despair, etc. This joy has an intellectual aspect and differs in kind from relatively simple sensuous pleasure.

It would be inaccurate to assume that physical pleasure, sonorous delight, is essential to the hearing of music. At different epochs, with different composers, it has played a role more or less important; but it is impossible to see here the *sine qua non* of esthetic emotion, any more than for the other arts. Certain composers offer us this pleasure of the senses, but the productions of others are cold and austere and seem to tend towards an ascetic art from which all physical voluptuousness would be banished . . .

But here we are in the domain of personal taste, of subjective impressions and judgments which allow of no discussion: this or that composer whose sonorities ravish our ears will seem to others dry, hard and painful. And the very composer who offered us only severe, intellectual joys seems suddenly a sensual enchanter, and vice versa . . . In a word, the sonorous delight which certain composers dispense so generously and others seem on principle to avoid (without always succeeding), is an unstable and capricious thing. In any case it would be as ridiculous to banish it from music on the pretext that it degrades (the sensuous charm of a *Nocturne* by Chopin or of a *Prelude* by Debussy does not at all weaken the spiritual significance of these passages) as it would be to insist that it be always present, denying all esthetic value to works which are not ingratiating

Musical emotion then, can develop in the absence of all sensuous pleasure, and even when the first hearing is painful. But is even this pleasure an immediate sensation, pure of all intellectual alloy? Is it of the same order as the pleasure a well prepared dish affords us?

Experience and reason alike show us that the pleasures of sound are but faintly analogous with the pleasures of taste, of touch or of smell, since they involve a comprehension of the work from which they derive. In order that music afford us a sensuous physical pleasure, we must first have understood it. This pleasure, supposedly simple and direct, is the result of the intellectual grasp of a sequence; to delight in a succession of sounds, a melody, as we delight in a well-cooked dish, we must apprehend the relations between these sounds. The physical charm of a Debussy, for example, can be felt only when one begins to find one's bearings in his music; and there undoubtedly are still people for whom the *Cathedrale Engloutie* is nothing but a chaotic medley of chords, who will never find in it any delight. If some sonorous combination happens to tickle their ears agreeably, the next chord, for them unrelated to the preceding, will immediately shatter the charm. For the person who understands, on the contrary, the pleasure is born precisely of this passing from one sonority to another, each acquiring its whole value only in relation with those which precede and follow The pleasure an uncomprehending auditor may happen to find in one or another of these chords does not differ essentially from the pleasure afforded us sometimes by the vibration of a telegraph wire, the murmur of a brook, etc. It is not a specifically musical, esthetic pleasure; it is merely one of the more or less agreeable sensations which our environment often offers, sensations that awaken vague images, fugitive emotions, and conspire to keep us in a certain state of well-being but which have nothing at all to do with art.

VI

If I dwell so insistently upon the distinction to be made between the complex reactions of those who hear a musical work and the act by which they grasp the meaning immanent in its sonorous body, this is because the attention of critics and estheticians is ordinarily concentrated upon these individual reactions in an effort to determine the laws which govern them. These laws exist, perhaps; for the constant physiological and psychological action of certain intervals and certain timbres seems indubitable. We are familiar with the theories so widespread today, which hold the musical work to be an ensemble of dynamic schemes acting upon us according to a definite rhythm: tension-resolution. There is certainly truth in these theories, but it cannot be too often repeated that psycho-physiological experiments and considerations neglect exactly those esthetic facts which most need explanation; the specific element which distinguishes our reactions to a musical work from those which the flux of real life provides.

For the rest, we must recognize that a large portion of a concert audience, a much larger one even than we think, does not listen to music, does not even know what it means to listen to music: for them music is merely a stimulant which plunges them into vague reveries to which they abandon themselves more or less unconsciously. It would greatly surprise impassioned "amateurs" to be told that to listen to a work is to be active, to accomplish a task sometimes actually painful, demanding a certain preparation, and that their exclusively passive attitude towards the sonorous text prevents them not only from grasping its meaning, but also from enjoying the specific pleasure it might have imparted had they followed attentively, instead of giving themselves up, like opium smokers, to the play of their imaginations.

It would be false, nevertheless, to conclude from this that the comprehension of music necessarily demands a knowledge of musical technic and that it is impossible to appreciate a musical work, to grasp its meaning, without possessing the elements of what one might call the musical grammar. There is an ambiguity here, it seems to me, which it is absolutely essential to dissipate. To understand a page of music—a sonata by Beethoven, a rondo by Mozart, a fugue by Bach—is not the same thing as to be able to make a technical analysis of these pages. One may understand form, harmony and counterpoint and still remain deaf to the work of which every element is perceived and named. I do not say that a knowledge of musical technic does not aid in comprehension; but we do have two absolutely different operations here.

The history of music and of musical criticism proves this to us conclusively. It is needless, I suppose, to cite examples of the total lack of comprehension often exhibited by the most learned theoreticians when confronted by musical productions which they were nevertheless perfectly capable of analyzing step by step. And we may remember on the other hand the discoveries made in music by men wholly without technical knowledge: it was not the conservatory professors who discovered Wagner, Debussy and Stravinsky for us. One may be an excellent grammarian, and still be at a loss before a sentence of this or that obscure writer—even though one can perfectly well point out the subject, the verb, the complement. But in ordinary language the words and their relations have a symbolic character; there is nothing surprising then in the fact that grammatical analysis is sometimes insufficient to give us immediately the logical significance of a sentence: if the meaning of but one sign escapes us the sentence no longer has any sense for us, no matter how clear it may be syntactically. Now since it is conceded that a musical work is not a sign, it is then pertinent to ask why its structure does not give us its meaning directly, and why, moreover, its meaning is often revealed to those incapable of analyzing the work formally.

This difficulty is superficial only; it is obviated as soon as we examine the problem closely. To understand a melody, a phrase, a musical work, is to perceive its unity; in other words, we understand a series of sounds when we succeed in making of this series a system, a coherent whole. And it is in this whole alone that each of the moments of the sonorous flow which we follow so attentively acquires its full value and its reality. The difference between the man who understands music and the man who does not, is simply this: the first perceives a system of complex relations, the second perceives only isolated sounds. For him who comprehends, an isolated sound is only an abstraction; the reality is the system which integrates these sounds.

An organism is not a mere composite of two arms, two legs, a torso, etc.; these very members exist only in an individual whole and as functions of this whole. In the same way the slightest melody is not a mere composite of sounds disposed in a certain order, according to a certain rhythm, but is an entity of a particular sort, unique, inimitable, lending its essential character to each of the elements which analysis reveals. Just as the word *luxe* in the celebrated verse of Baudelaire possesses unique sonority and a significance absolutely different from what it might have in a fashion report, so the sound which we call *do* changes altogether in passing from one musical composition to another; we may say, in brief, that we are never dealing with the same sounds and that there are as many *do's* and *re's* etc., as there are musical organisms.

This sonorous flood which vanishes as soon as it is born we grasp, in so far as we understand it, as a certain stable, definite and objective reality. But this reality does not transcend the sound: it is what constitutes their immanent unity, what gives them a precise significance. We see now why analyzing a musical work is not the same thing as understanding it. Technical analysis gives us at best only the abstract formula of a work, and thus reduces it to a certain type; while to understand a piece of music is to recreate its unique personality as it first emerged in the mind of the composer.

This recreation does not require a memory capable of retaining the whole of the work from beginning to end, something very few can do. The synthesis proceeds progressively, moving with the flood of sound, each moment of which thus bears, in a sense, the accumulated burden of the preceding moments —not because we *remember* them, but because we perceive each of them as direct functions of those which have preceded. Having come to the end of the piece, we have perhaps forgotten the beginning and might in any case be unable to reconstruct it, but the work well understood is found again and exists integrally in the concluding chord: a person entering the hall at this moment would hear merely a simple perfect chord, but for the rest of us who have integrated it in a definite system it possesses a specific sonorous value.

If we regard the matter from this point of view, the diversity of reactions among an audience in the presence of a musical work and the varying avatars into which different interpreters shape this music at various times does not at all affect its integrity: what makes an organism of it, what constitutes its formal unity, exists always. *In so far as they have grasped this unity, in so far as they have perceived the work as a complex whole, the auditors,* whatever may be their secondary reactions, *will understand it in the same way; it will reveal the same thing to them, namely, what it is.* Only the secondary reactions change. It is cerain that today, before a *Passion* by Bach, for example, we have other emotions, other thoughts than had the contemporaries of Bach and the composer himself; but there is only one way of understanding it.

THE BAROQUE ERA

2

Donald Jay Grout

1902-

CHARACTERISTICS OF THE BAROQUE

Donald Jay Grout is a musicologist who teaches at Cornell University. In addition to *A History of Western Music* (1960), selections from which are included here, he has written *A Short History of Opera*.

THE WORD *Baroque* has recently been brought into the vocabulary of music history to designate both a chronological period extending from about the end of the sixteenth century to the middle of the eighteenth, and the style of music typical of that period. As with other epochs, the boundary dates are only approximations, since many characteristics of Baroque music were in evidence before 1600 and many were disappearing before 1750. But it is possible and convenient to take these dates as the approximate limits within which certain ways of organizing musical material, certain ideals of musical sound, and certain kinds of musical expression developed from diverse and scattered beginnings to an assured and workable system, exemplified at its highest in the works of Johann Sebastian Bach and of George Frideric Handel.

What are the characteristics of Baroque music? To answer this question, we must consider how that music is related to the surroundings which produced it. The use of the term *Baroque* to describe the music of 1600-1750 suggests that historians believe its qualities are in some ways similar to the qualities of contemporary architecture, painting, literature, and perhaps also science and philosophy. We must believe that a connection exists, not only in the seventeenth century, but in all eras, between music and the other creative activities of man: that the music produced in any age must reflect, in terms appropriate to its own nature, the same conceptions and tendencies that are expressed in other arts contemporary with it. For this reason general labels like *Baroque, Gothic,* and *Romantic* are often used in music history instead of designations that might more precisely describe purely musical characteristics. It is true that these general words are liable to be misunderstood. Thus *Baroque,* which perhaps comes from a Portuguese word meaning "of irregular shape," was long used in the pejorative sense of "abnormal, bizarre, exaggerated, in bad taste, grotesque"; the word is still defined thus in the dictionaries, and still carries at least some of that meaning for many people. However, the music written between 1600 and 1750 is not on the whole any more abnormal, fantastic, or grotesque than that of any other period, and the pejorative connotations of *Baroque* do not apply to it.

Baroque music was dominated by Italian ideas. From the mid-sixteenth to the mid-eighteenth centuries, Italy remained the most influential musical nation of Europe. One should say *region* rather than *nation,* for the Italian peninsula was split into areas ruled by Spain and Austria, as well as a half-dozen smaller independent states which allied themselves from time to time with larger European powers and in general heartily distrusted one another. Yet political sickness apparently does not preclude artistic health: Venice was a leading musical city all through the seventeenth century despite her political impotence, and the same was true of Naples during most of the eighteenth century. Rome exerted a steady influence on sacred music and for a time in the seventeenth century was an important center of opera and cantata; Florence had her brilliant period near the beginning of the seventeenth century.

As for the other European countries during the Baroque era, France after 1650 developed a national style of music which resisted Italian influences for over a hundred years. In Germany the already weakened musical culture of the sixteenth century was overwhelmed by the calamity of the Thirty Years' War (1618-48), but despite political disunity there was a mighty resurgence in the following generations, climaxing in Johann Sebastian Bach. In England the glories of the Elizabethan and Jacobean ages faded with the period of the Civil War and the Commonwealth (1642-60); a brief brilliant revival toward the end of the century was followed by complete capitulation to Italian style.

The musical primacy of Italy during the Baroque was not absolute, but even in the countries that developed and maintained their own distinctive national idiom the Italian influence could not be escaped. It was prominent in France through the first half of the seventeenth century especially; the composer whose works did most to establish the national French style after 1660, Jean-Baptiste Lully, was an Italian by birth. In Germany in the latter part of the century, Italian style was the principal foundation on which German composers built; even the art of Bach owed much to Italy, and Handel's work was as much Italian as German. By the end of the Baroque period, in fact, the music of Europe had become an international language with Italian roots. . . .

Despite continuous evolution, certain musical features remained constant throughout the Baroque era. One of these was a distinction drawn between two styles of composition. This distinction did not describe a diversity of individual idioms within one common style, nor even a diversity of manner between simpler and more complex types of writing, such as had existed in the sixteenth century, for example, between the frottolo and the ballett on the one hand and the madrigal on the other. It was rather an acknowledged stylistic dichotomy, which writers of the time differentiated in various ways. In 1605 Monteverdi called these opposing styles *prima prattica* and *seconda prattica,* or the first and second "practices." By the first he meant the style of the Netherlanders which had culminated in the work of Willaert; and by the second he meant the style of the modern Italians such as de Rore, Marenzio, and himself. The basis of the distinction for Monteverdi was that in the first practice music dominated the text, whereas in the second practice the text dominated the music; hence it followed that in the new style the old rules might be modified and, in particular, dissonances might be used freely to make the music conform to the expression of feeling in the text. Other writers called the two practices *stile antico* and *stile moderno* (old and modern style), or *stylus gravis* and *stylus luxurians* (sober and ornamented style); this last designation implied the use of fast notes, unusual skips, and a well-marked melody, as well as dissonances. In short, the difference came to about what we today call "strict style" and "free style." The older style was considered appropriate for church, although not all church compositions were by any means written in it. Nor were the two styles always kept separate in practice.

Another characteristic of Baroque music was that composers began to be attracted by the idea of writing music specifically for a particular medium, such as the violin or the solo voice, rather than music that might be either sung or played or performed by almost any combination of voices and instruments, as could many pieces composed in the sixteenth century. The violin family began to replace the older viols, and composers developed an idiomatic violin style; also the art of singing, promoted by famous teachers and virtuosi, advanced very rapidly in the seventeenth century. Instrumental and vocal styles began to be differentiated; eventually they became so distinct that in the later Baroque composers consciously used vocal idioms in instrumental writing, and vice versa.

One trait common to all Baroque composers was the effort they made to express, or rather represent, a wide range of ideas and feelings with the utmost vividness and vehemence by means of music. This effort was, in a way, an extension of the Renaissance idea of *musica reservata*. But whereas in the sixteenth century the emotions represented were relatively restricted and the presentation was held within the bounds of an aristocratic concept of moderation and detachment, in the Baroque these barriers were down. Composers struggled to find musical language for extreme *affections* or states of the soul, such as rage, excitement, grandeur, heroism, lofty contemplation, wonder, or mystic exaltation, and to intensify these musical effects by means of violent contrasts. In Baroque architecture, sculpture, and painting the normal forms of objects were sometimes distorted, as though past the natural limits of the medium, to reflect the passionate intensity of the artist's thought; in Baroque music, also, the limits of the old order of consonance and dissonance, of regular and equable rhythmic flow, were being broken down. But music, since it is not conditioned, as are sculpture and painting, by the necessity of representing natural objects nor, as is architecture, by the unyielding physical properties of the medium and a functional character, is able to expand in whatever directions the imagination of a composer may suggest. In fact, such expansion is natural to music; and in the seventeenth century it was an important stimulus both to the development of music itself and also to its increasing relative importance.

The music of the Baroque was thus not written to express the feelings of an individual artist, but to represent affections; these were not communicated haphazardly or left to individual intuition, but were conveyed by means of a systematic, regulated vocabulary, a common repertory of musical *figures* or devices. Figures were suggested by or borrowed from other arts, particularly rhetoric and poetry; they were of diverse sorts and were diversely combined, but their use meant that the music of the Baroque was a language capable of depicting not only affections, but even to some extent also images and objects of the external world. This aspect of Baroque music is not of fundamental importance, since the success of any composition ultimately depends on its inherent musical content and not on its depiction of extra-musical matters. The depictive intention in many Baroque compositions must not be disregarded; but neither must it be over-emphasized, as many Romantic writers in the nineteenth century tended to over-emphasize it with respect to the music of Bach.

Diversity of styles and idioms, together with the effort made to represent vividly and precisely ideas and feelings, brought into Baroque music factors that were somewhat incompatible. Baroque music shows conflict and tension between the centrifugal forces of freedom of expression and the constructive forces of discipline and order in a musical composition. This tension, always latent in any work of art, was eventually made overt and consciously exploited by Baroque musicians; and this acknowledged dualism is the most important characteristic which distinguishes between the music of this period and that of the Renaissance. The dualism is apparent in the existence of the two practices. It is also evident in the two ways the Baroque treated rhythm: (1) regular metrical barline rhythm on the one hand; and (2) free unmetrical rhythm, used in recitative or improvisatory solo instrumental pieces, on the other.

Regular dance rhythms were, of course, known in the Renaissance; but not until the seventeenth century did most music begin to be written and heard in *measures*—definite patterns of strong and weak beats. At first these patterns were not regularly recurring; the use of a single time signature corresponding to a regular succession of harmonic and accentual patterns, set off by barlines at regular intervals, was common only after 1650. By the late Baroque, it had become customary for a composer to establish a distinctive rhythmic pattern at the beginning of a composition or movement, and to hold predominantly to this basic pattern throughout; the piece thus represented a single "basic affection," and made only sparing use of contrasting material.

Along with strictly measured rhythm, Baroque composers also used an irregular, inconstant, flexible rhythm in writing instrumental toccatas and vocal recitatives. Obviously the two rhythms could not be used simultaneously; but they were frequently used successively for deliberate contrast, as in the customary pairing of toccata and fugue or recitative and aria.

The basic sound ideal of the Renaissance was a polyphony of equal independent voices; the sound ideal of the Baroque was a firm bass and a florid treble, held together by unobtrusive harmony. The idea of a musical texture consisting of a single melody supported by accompanying harmonies was not in itself new; something like it had been used in the ballade style of the *ars nova,* in the Burgundian chanson, in the early frottola, in the sixteenth-century lute songs, and in the Elizabethan ayre. The ideas that were new in the Baroque were the emphasis on the bass, the isolation of the bass and treble as the two essential lines of the texture, and the seeming indifference to the inner voice lines. This indifference was perfectly pictured in a system of notation used during the Baroque, called the *thoroughbass* or *basso continuo:* the composer wrote out the melody and the bass; the bass was played on one or more *fundament* or *continuo* instruments (clavier, organ, lute), usually reinforced by a sustaining instrument such as a bass gamba or violoncello or bassoon; and above the bass notes the keyboard or lute player filled in the required chords, which were not otherwise written out. . . .

The *realization*—the actual playing—of such a *figured bass* varied according to the nature of the composition and the taste and skill of the player; he might play simple chords, introduce passing tones or other ornaments, or incorporate melodic motives in imitation of the trebel or bass parts. (A modern edition of compositions with a figured bass usually indicates in smaller notes the editor's conception of a proper realization.) The realization of the basso continuo was not always essential: that is to say, many pieces were provided with a continuo even though all the notes necessary for the full harmony were already present in the notated melodic vocal or instrumental parts. In motets or madrigals for four or five voices, for example, the continuo instrument actually did no more than double or support the voices. But for solos and duets the continuo was usually necessary to complete the harmonies as well as to produce a fuller sonority.

It might seem that the Baroque basso continuo implied a total rejection of the kind of counterpoint written in the sixteenth century and earlier. As a matter of fact, this was true when the continuo was used alone as accompaniment to a solo, unless the composer chose to give the bass line itself some melodic significance, for the thoroughbass *was* a radical departure from all previous methods of writing music. But it must be remembered that a firm bass and florid treble was not the only kind of musical texture in the Baroque. For a long time, composers continued to write unaccompanied motets and madrigals; some instrumental ensemble pieces, as well as all solo keyboard and lute music, made no use of the basso continuo; most important, even in ensembles where the continuo was used, counterpoint did not disappear. But the new counterpoint of the seventeenth century was different from that of the Renaissance. It was still a blending of different melodic lines, but the lines all had to fit into the regulative framework of a series of harmonic chord progressions explicitly defined and sounded by the continuo: it was, in short, a harmonically governed counterpoint, whose melodies were subordinated to the harmonic scheme.

Within the harmonies thus defined, composers eventually were able to use dissonance quite freely, just because the underlying harmonies were so clear. Much dissonance in the early seventeenth century was experimental; toward the middle of the century dissonance almost disappeared; then, in the last part of the Baroque, it returned, incorporated in a complex system of tonal organization. . . .

That system was the major-minor tonality familiar to us in the music of the eighteenth and nineteenth centuries: all the harmonies of a composition organized in relation to a triad on the key note or tonic supported primarily by triads on its dominant and subdominant with other chords secondary to these, and with temporary modulations to other keys allowed without sacrificing the supremacy of the principal key. This particular tonal organization had long been foreshadowed; it was implicit in much music of the Renaissance, especially that written in the latter half of the sixteenth century. Rameau's *Treatise on Harmony* (1722) completed the theoretical formulation of the system, but it had existed in practice for at least forty years before.

3

Manfred Bukofzer

1910-1955

BAROQUE STYLE

(Selections from *Music in the Baroque Era*)

The musicologist, Manfred Bukofzer, lectured and taught in Basel, Oxford, Cambridge, and California. His numerous publications include studies in medieval, Renaissance, and Baroque music. *Music in the Baroque Era* was published in 1947.

Baroque and Renaissance—Comparison of styles

MANY ATTEMPTS HAVE BEEN MADE to bring the contrast of renaissance and baroque music down to a short formula. In Renaissance music, "harmony is the master of the word"; in Baroque music "the word is the master of harmony." This neat antithesis, which merely paraphrases Monteverdi's distinction of first and second practice, touches, indeed, upon one fundamental aspect of Baroque music, the musical expression of the text or what was called, at the time, *expressio verborum*. That term does not have the modern, emotional connotation of "expressive music" and can more accurately be rendered as "musical representation of the word." The means of verbal representation in Baroque music were not direct, psychological, and emotional, but indirect, that is, intellectual and pictorial. The modern psychology of dynamic emotions did not yet exist in the Baroque era. Feelings were classified and stereotyped in a set of so-called affections, each representing a mental state which was in itself static. It was the business of the composer to make the affection of the music correspond to that of the words.

According to the lucid rationalism of the time, the composer had at his disposal a set of musical figures which were pigeonholed like the affections themselves and were designed to represent these affections in music.

The Renaissance favored the affections of restraint and noble simplicity, the Baroque the extreme affections, ranging from violent pain to exuberant joy. It is obvious that the representation of extreme affections called for a richer vocabulary than had been required before. The Renaissance artist saw in music a self-contained autonomous art, subject only to its own laws. The Baroque artist saw in music a heteronomous art, subordinated to words and serving only as musical means to a dramatic end that transcended music.

The most striking difference between Renaissance and Baroque music comes to light in the treatment of dissonance. The Baroque dissonance treatment depended upon a voice able to carry chords, and consequently the bass received more attention than ever before. Indeed the peculiar form in which the bass was made to serve the new function was as characteristic of the Baroque period as its name: THOROUGH-BASS, or *bass continuo*. The presence of the continuo is a clear indication of Baroque style, and its absence, aside from keyboard works, is so exceptional as to require a special note by the composer.

At the beginning of the Baroque period, a novel stylistic element made its appearance: IDIOMATIC WRITING. The Baroque era consciously developed the idiomatic possibilities inherent in the instrumental and vocal media. The idiom-consciousness of the Baroque era must be understood as another aspect of its style-consciousness, and nowhere does the difference between Renaissance and Baroque music come more openly to the surface than here. The Renaissance conception of musical structure was premised upon part-writing which embraced vocal and instrumental music alike. By its very nature this conception did not stress musical styles idiomatic for particular instruments, and consequently the voices of Renaissance music could be performed vocally or instrumentally, or, conversely, instrumental parts were often designated "to be played or sung" although no words were given. The fact that voice or instrument were interchangeable shows how strongly the emphasis rested not on the medium, but on the realization of the single parts. . . .

It was the Baroque composer who developed the idiomatic characteristics of voice and instrument, and it was he who deployed them first in the CONCERTATO[1] style of the early Baroque. The idiomatic possibilities of the solo voice were explored in the remarkable virtuoso singing of the early Baroque, and then crystallized in the refined methods of the Italian *bel canto*. Vocal and instrumental ensembles sharpened the ear for the difference of vocal and instrumental idioms, consciously juxtaposed in opera, oratorio, and cantata. After Gabrieli and Schütz the choral idiom was distinctly divorced from that of the solo ensemble. The instruments, especially, gradually developed specific styles, notably the violin family, and to a lesser degree the wind instruments. Lute and keyboard music, too, became more idiomatic than before, and composers showed great resourcefulness in taking advantage of the peculiar aptitudes and weaknesses of the respective instruments. Nobody can mistake the violin character of a concerto grosso by Vivaldi, which was conceived from the outset in this medium.

With the discovery of idioms in the Baroque, new possibilities arose from the deliberate exchange of idioms between different instruments, or between instrument and voice. The transfer of idioms forms one of the most fascinating aspects of Baroque music. Lute ornaments could be transferred to the harpsichord, vocal techniques could be imitated by the violin, and violin figuration could appear in organ music. In the late Baroque a rich interchange and interpretation of idioms can be ob-

[1] "The concertato style . . . is one in which different musical elements are engaged not on a completely cooperative basis, as in counterpoint or monody, but in a manner which deliberately emphasizes the contrast of one voice or instrument against another, or of one group against another, or of a group against a solo." D. J. Grout, *A History of Western Music*, p. 285.

served which reached almost incredible complexity.

A great variety of forms, techniques, and idioms was created in the Baroque era for the first time in music history, providing a fund of musical material that has survived in various transformations to the present day. The Baroque saw the first development of the opera, the oratorio, and the cantata; and the creation of the solo sonata, the trio sonata, and the chamber duet. It was the age of the prelude and fugue, the chorale prelude, and the chorale fantasy. It instituted the important forms of the concerto grosso and the solo concerto. The Baroque reached the first peak in the history of opera in the works of Scarlatti and Handel, the first peak of the concerto in the works of Vivaldi and Bach, and the first peak of the oratorio in the works of Handel. The Baroque created the unique dramatic *concertato* style of which Gabrieli, Monteverdi, and Schütz were the leading masters. It represents, finally, in the works of Bach, the greatest period of organ music, and likewise the greatest period of Protestant church music.

The Baroque style went through several phases that do not even coincide in different countries. They can be grouped into three major periods: early, middle, and late Baroque. Although the periods actually overlap in time, they can roughly be dated as follows: the first from 1580 to 1630, the second from 1630 to 1680, and the last from 1680 to 1730. These spans indicate only the formative periods of the new concepts with which the previous ones may run parallel for some time. It must also be clearly understood that the dates apply only to Italy, from which Baroque music received its main impulses. In the other countries, the respective periods began about ten or twenty years later than in Italy. Thus it becomes understandable that around 1730, when Italy had already turned to the *style galant,* Germany brought Baroque music to its consummation.

A short characterization of the three periods will serve to elucidate their important differences with regard to style. In early Baroque style two ideas prevailed: the opposition to counterpoint and the most violent interpretation of the words, realized in the affective recitative in free rhythm. With it appeared an extraordinary desire for dissonance. The harmony was experimental and pre-tonal, that is, its chords were not yet tonally directed. For this reason the power to sustain a longer movement was lacking, and in consequence all forms were on a small scale and sectional. The differentiation of vocal and instrumental idioms began, vocal music being in the leading position.

The middle Baroque period brought above all the *bel-canto* style in the cantata and opera, and with it the distinction between aria and recitative. The single sections of musical forms began to grow and contrapuntal texture was reinstituted. The modes were reduced to major and minor, and the chord progressions were governed by a rudimentary tonality which restrained the free dissonance treatment of the early Baroque. Vocal and instrumental music were of equal importance.

The Late Baroque

The late Baroque style is distinguished by a fully established tonality which regulated chord progressions, dissonance treatment, and the formal structure. The contrapuntal technique culminated in the full absorption of tonal harmony. The forms grew to large dimensions. The concerto style appeared and with it the emphasis on mechanical rhythm. The exchange of idioms reached its highest point. Vocal music was dominated by instrumental music. Tonality established a gradated system of chordal relations between a tonal center (the tonic triad in major or minor) and the other triads (or seventh chords) of the diatonic scale. None of these chords was in itself new, but they now served a new function, namely that of circumscribing the key. It is no mere metaphor if tonality is explained in terms of gravitation. Both tonality and gravitation were discoveries of the Baroque period made at exactly the same time.

Tonality provided also a framework of harmony able to sustain large forms. It set up harmonic goals without which the extended forms of late Baroque music would not have been possible. It gave a new perspective to the two structural voices of the composition. In the relation between melody and chord progression the consideration of the latter began to weigh more heavily than the former. The melodies were increasingly conditioned by and dependent on the harmonic accompaniment.

With the final consolidation of style, the establishment of tonality, luxuriant counterpoint, and continuo-homophony, definite formal patterns emerged which usually pass as the forms of Baroque music in general. Actually they characterize only late baroque music. The church sonata crystallized as a four-movement form in the order of slow-fast-slow-fast. It can be found not only in solo and trio sonatas, but also in certain concerti grossi and Italian overtures. The suite also assumed, at least in German music, the features of a four-movement form in the order of allemande, courante, saraband, and gigue, though it could be expanded by inserted dances. The main type of three-movement form in the order of fast-slow-fast was represented by the concerto.

While the movements of the cycle followed a fixed scheme the internal organization of the single movement depended on a highly flexible formal principle. Since late Baroque music was essentially monothematic and continuously developed a short motive, it has often been considered as "formless." The continuity of late Baroque music was correctly observed, but its interpretation as a "formless" process was obviously tainted by the conception of development in the classic sonata form. The late Baroque type of development lacked the dramatic and psychological qualities of the sonata and must be clearly distinguished from the classic type. It is best defined as "continuous expansion." Being a formal principle and not a scheme, it lent itself to infinite variation as to formal patterns.

In its most consistent manifestation, continuous expansion produced a movement that elaborated a single motive in an unbroken series of rhythmic figures, running from beginning to end without a break like a *perpetuum mobile*. More commonly, however, there were several incisions in the movement. The motive was distinctly stated and then consistently expanded in modulatory fashion; when a new key had been confirmed by a cadence the same beginning was restated in the new key, further expanded, and so on to the end.

Composer and Audience

The fatal gap between composer and audience that characterizes modern musical life did not exist in the Baroque period. The composers wrote as a matter of course in an idiom that was "modern" at the time. They did not fear, as our contemporary composers sometimes do, that their genius might be recognized only after they had been safely dead long enough to be recognized as "classics." The aristocrats and the patricians had sufficient technical training in music to keep abreast with the musical innovations of the time. This high level of musical understanding was taken for granted although the unschooled common people were obviously far removed from it. In view of the restricted social background of Baroque music it is not surprising that the common man was given no consideration. Complaints that the common people did not understand the elaborate church music were quite frequent. It is interesting to see how these justified objections were countered. In his *Psalmodia Christiana* Mithobius disposed of the argument in a highly significant fashion. He admitted that the common man was unable to understand "all tricks and artifices of the musician," but he did not conclude from this fact that music should be composed on a lower level within the grasp of the untrained. He maintained on the contrary that the common people should rise to the music by "exercise" because the more labor and artifice was devoted to the praise of God the better: "God cannot be praised artificially enough." Even though the people did not quite follow the composer, it was, according to Mithobius, enough for them to know that a sacred piece was being performed. He clearly disclosed the strong ethical reason why patterned elaborations and contrapuntal complexity held so central a place in music. It did not occur to the composers to "write down" to an audience, nor were they bothered by the idea of writing for eternity. Bach's works were composed for the various occasions of the liturgical year and these called for his best efforts. Precisely because Bach wrote for the day as elaborately and "artificially" as he could, he composed music that was not of an age, but for all time.

4

Johann Joachim Quantz

1697-1773

JUDGING MUSIC

Quantz achieved fame as a flute player and composer for
Frederick the Great, and for his treatise on playing the flute
which was published in 1752. This work does not confine itself
merely to a discussion of flute playing, as the excerpts given
below illustrate.

THERE IS PERHAPS NO ART so subject to every man's judgment as
music. It would seem as though there were nothing easier than
to judge it. Not only every musician, but also everyone who
gives himself out as a musical amateur, wishes likewise to be
regarded as a judge of what he hears.

Now since music is the sort of art which must be judged, not
according to our own fancy, but, like the other fine arts, according to good taste, acquired through certain rules and refined by
much experience and exercise; since he who wishes to judge
another ought to understand at least as much as the other, if
not more; since these qualities are seldom met with in those who
occupy themselves with the judging of music; since, on the contrary, the greater part of these are governed by ignorance, prejudice, and passions which hinder correct judgment; many a one
would do much better if he would keep his judgment to himself
and listen with greater attention, if, without judging, he can
still take pleasure in music.

In judging music, besides obeying the usual dictates of reason
and fairness, we should always pay particular attention to three

points, namely, to the piece itself, to the performer, and to the listener. A fine composition may be mutilated by a bad performance; a poor composition, on the other hand, deprives the performer of his advantage; we must first determine, therefore, whether it is the performer or the composition that is responsible for the good or bad effect. With regard to the listener, as with regard to the performer, much depends on the various constitutions of the temperament. Some prefer the magnificent and lively style, some the mournful and profound, some the gay and delicate; each is governed by his inclinations. Some have considerable knowledge which others lack. We are not always carried away immediately the first time we hear this piece or that. It often happens that a piece pleases us today which tomorrow, if we chance to be in a different mood, we can scarcely sit through; on the other hand, a piece may displease us today in which tomorrow we discover beauties. A piece may be well written and well played; even so it fails to please everyone. A poor piece badly played may displease many; at the same time it finds a few admirers. The place in which a piece of music is performed can put many obstacles in the way of our judging it correctly. We hear, for example, one and the same piece, today from near by, tomorrow from far off. In each case we notice a difference. We may hear a piece intended for a vast place and a large orchestra in its proper setting. It will please us immensely. But if, at some other time, we hear the same piece in a room, performed perhaps by other persons, with a few instruments accompanying, it will have lost half its beauty. A piece that has well-nigh enchanted us in the chamber may be barely recognizable when we hear it in the theater. Each piece, then, must be played in the style that belongs to it; unless this is done, there can be no judgment.

After this, everyone will grant me, I believe, that the correct and impartial judgment of a piece of music requires, not merely a little insight, but perhaps the highest degree of musical skill;

that far more is involved than merely being able to sing or play a little ourselves; and that, as a result of this, if we would judge, we must apply ourselves assiduously to the attainment of that knowledge which reason, good taste, and art have placed within our reach. And further, I hope that no one will wish to dispute my contention that not every one of those who commonly set themselves up as judges of music is equipped with this knowledge and that, for this reason, there must arise a great detriment to music, musicians, and musical amateurs, who are kept thereby in a constant state of uncertainty. . . .

A concerto grosso consists in a mixture of various concerted instruments wherein, as an invariable rule, two or more parts—the number may sometimes run as high as eight or even higher—concert with one another. In the concerto da camera, however, there is only a single concerted instrument.

The qualities of a concerto grosso require, in each of its movements: (1) a magnificent ritornello at the beginning, which should be more harmonic than melodic, more serious than humorous, and relieved by unisons; (2) a skillful mixture of the imitations in the concerted parts, in order that the ear may be unexpectedly surprised, now by this instrument, now by that; (3) these imitations must be made up of short and pleasing ideas; (4) there must be a constant alternation of the brilliant and the ingratiating; (5) the inner tutti sections must be kept short; (6) the alternations of the concerted instruments must be so distributed that one is not heard too much and another too little; (7) now and then, after a trio, there must be woven in a short solo for one instrument or another; (8) before the end the solo instruments must briefly repeat what they had at the beginning; and (9) the final tutti must conclude with the loftiest and most magnificent ideas of the first ritornello. Such a concerto requires numerous accompanying players, a large place, a serious performance, and a moderate tempo.

For the arousing and subsequent stilling of the passions the Adagio offers greater opportunity than the Allegro. In former times it was for the most part written in a plain dry style, more harmonic than melodic. The composers left to the performers what had been expected of them, namely, to make the melody singable, but this could not be well accomplished without considerable addition of embellishments. In other words, it was in those days much easier to write an Adagio than to play one. Now, as it may be readily imagined that such an Adagio did not always have the good fortune to fall into skillful hands, and since the performance was seldom as successful as the author might have wished, there has come of this evil some good, namely, that composers have for some time past begun to make their Adagios more singing. By this means the composer has more honor and the performer less of a puzzle; moreover, the Adagio itself can no longer be distorted or mutilated in such a variety of ways as was formerly often the case.

The final Allegro of a concerto must be very different from the first movement, not only in its style and nature, but also in its meter. The last Allegro must be just as humorous and gay as the first is serious. In no case should all three movements of a concerto be written in the same meter. And although the last movement is in the key of the first, the composer, to avoid similarity in the modulations, must still be careful not to pass through the same succession of keys in the last movement as he did in the first. Generally speaking, in the last movement (1) The ritornello must be short, gay, fiery, but at the same time somewhat playful. (2) The principal part must have a simple melody, pleasing and fleeting. (3) The solo passages should be easy, in order that the rapidity of the movement may not be impeded. They may, further, bear no similarity to those in the first movement.

5

Jean-Philippe Rameau

1683-1764

ON THE PROPERTIES OF HARMONY

In his *Treatise on Harmony* (1727) , Jean-Philippe Rameau, composer and theoretician, provided the basis for the harmonic structure of most eighteenth- and nineteenth-century music. This selection is from Chapter 20 of the *Treatise*.

IT IS CERTAIN that harmony can arouse in us different passions, depending on the particular harmonies that are employed. There are harmonies that are sad, languishing, tender, agreeable, gay, and striking; there are also certain successions of harmonies for the expression of these passions; and although it is quite foreign to my purpose I shall give of this as full an explanation as experience has given me.

Consonant harmonies are to be found everywhere but should be employed most frequently in music expressing gaiety and magnificence; and, since we cannot avoid intermingling some dissonant harmonies, we must contrive that these arise naturally, that they are as far as possible prepared, and that the most prominent parts, the soprano and bass, are always consonant with respect to one another.

Sweetness and tenderness are sometimes well enough expressed by prepared minor dissonances.

Languishings and sufferings are perfectly expressed by dissonances "by supposition" and especially by chromatic progressions. . . .

Despair and all passions having to do with anger or which have anything striking about them require unprepared dissonances of every kind; above all, the major dissonances should be situated in the soprano. In certain expressions of this nature it is even effective to pass from one key to another by means of unprepared major dissonances, yet in such a way that the ear is not offended by too great a disproportion; like all other such procedures, this can accordingly be carried out only with considerable discretion, for if we do nothing but pile dissonance on dissonance wherever there is place for it, it will be a much greater fault than allowing only consonance to be heard. Dissonance, then, is to be employed with considerable discretion, and, when we feel that its harshness is not in agreement with the expression, we ought even to avoid allowing it to be heard, in those harmonies that cannot do without it, by suppressing it adroitly, dispersing the consonances which make up the rest of the harmony through all the parts; for one ought always to bear in mind that the seventh, from which all the dissonances arise, is simply a sound added to the triad which does not at all destroy the basis of the harmony and may always be suppressed when we think it appropriate.

Melody has not less force than harmony in expression, but it is almost impossible to give certain rules for it, since good taste is here more influential than other considerations. Hence we leave to happy geniuses the pleasure of distinguishing themselves in this particular, the source of almost all the force of the sentiments, and hope that skillful persons, for whom we have said nothing new, will not resent our having revealed secrets of which they have wished, perhaps, to be the sole proprietors, for our limited intelligence does not permit us to rival them in this last degree of perfection, without which the most beautiful harmony becomes insipid and through which they are always in a position to excel.... It is only when we know how to arrange a series of harmonies appropriately that we can derive from them a melody suited to the subject, but taste is, in this, always the prime mover.

It is here that the ancients would appear to have excelled, if we may believe their accounts: one by his melody made Ulysses weep, another obliged Alexander to take up arms, still another rendered a furious young man mild and gentle. In a word, one sees on every hand the astonishing effects of their music, regarding which Zarlino is most plausible when he says that with them the word "harmony" often signified nothing more than simple melody and that all these effects arose more from an energetic discourse whose force was intensified by their manner of reciting or singing it and which can certainly not have enjoyed all the diversity which perfect harmony, of which they were ignorant, has obtained for us today. Their harmony, he says further, consisted only in a triad, which he calls a "symphony," above which they sang all sorts of melodies indifferently, very much like what is played on our musettes and vielles.

For the rest, a good musician ought to surrender himself to all the characters he wishes to depict and, like a skillful actor, put himself in the place of the speaker, imagine himself in the localities where the different events he wishes to represent occur, and take in these the same interest as those most concerned; he ought to be a good speaker, at least by nature; and he ought to know when the voice should be raised or lowered, by more or by less, in order to adapt to this his melody, his harmony, his modulation, and his movement.

6

Carl Philipp Emanuel Bach

1714-1788

ON PLAYING CONTINUO ACCOMPANIMENT AND
EMBELLISHMENTS

Third son of Johann Sebastian Bach, Carl Philipp Emanuel
achieved distinction as a performer on the harpsichord and
piano, and as a composer in the new styles that were precursors
of the Classical era. His *Essay on the True Art of Playing Keyboard Instruments,* first published in 1753, reflects the changing
taste in the use of improvisation.

THE ORGAN, HARPSICHORD, pianoforte, and clavichord are the
keyboard instruments most commonly used for continuo accompaniment. The organ is indispensible in church music with
its fugues, large choruses, and sustained style. It provides splen-
dor and maintains order. However, in all recitatives and arias
in this style, especially those in which a simple accompaniment
permits free variation on the part of the singer, a harpsichord
must be used. The emptiness of a performance without this
accompanying instrument is, unfortunately, made apparent to
us far too often. Thus, no piece can be well performed without
some form of keyboard accompaniment. Even in heavily scored
works, where no one would think that the harpsichord could be
heard, its absence can certainly be felt.

An accompanist must fit to each piece a correct performance
of its harmony in the proper volume with a suitable distribution
of tones. It is wrong to believe that the rules of good performance pertain only to the playing of solos. They must also be

observed in certain respects in fashioning an accompaniment. This latter has more elements which are concerned with the rules of good performance than solos have, for an accompanist is responsible for more than a correct realization of a bass; he must make intelligent adjustments with respect to the volume and register of chords.

The fewer the parts in a piece, the finer must be its accompaniment. Hence, a solo or an aria provides the best opportunity to judge an accompanist. He must take great pains to catch in his accompaniment all of the nuances of the principal part. Indeed, it is difficult to say whether accompanist or soloist deserves greater credit. The accompanist is usually given much less time; he is allowed only a cursory examination of the piece, but must nevertheless support and enhance extemporaneously all the beauty on which so much time and care have been expended by the principal performer. Yet the soloist takes all bravos to himself and gives no credit to his accompanist.

Gratuitous passage work and bustling noise do not constitute the beauties of accompaniment. In fact, they can easily do harm to the principal part by robbing it of its freedom to introduce variations into repetitions and elsewhere. The accompanist will achieve eminence and attract the attention of intelligent listeners by letting them hear an unadorned steadiness and noble simplicity in a flowing accompaniment which does not interfere with the brilliance of the principal parts. He need feel no anxiety over his being forgotten if he is not constantly joining in the tumult. No! An understanding listener does not easily miss anything. In his soul's perception melody and harmony are inseparable. Yet, should the opportunity arise and the nature of a piece permit it, when the principal part pauses or performs plain notes the accompanist may open the draft on his damped fire.

To accompany with discretion means moreover to make modifications in accord with certain liberties that are taken at times by the principal performer, who, without its being actually required, may depart somewhat from the written notes in introducing embellishments and variants.

No one disputes the need for embellishments. This is evident from the great numbers of them everywhere to be found. They are, in fact, indispensable. Consider their many uses: They connect and enliven tones and impart stress and accent; they make music pleasing and awaken our close attention. Expression is heightened by them; let a piece be sad, joyful, or otherwise, and they will lend a fitting assistance. Embellishments provide opportunities for fine performance as well as much of its subject matter. They improve mediocre compositions. Without them the best melody is empty and ineffective, the clearest content clouded.

In view of their many commendable services, it is unfortunate that there are also poor embellishments and that good ones are sometimes used too frequently and ineptly.

Because of this, it has always been better for composers to specify the proper embellishments unmistakably, instead of leaving their selection to the whims of tasteless performers.

In justice to the French it must be said that they notate their ornaments with painstaking accuracy. And so do the masters of the keyboard in Germany, but without embellishing to excess. Who knows but that our moderation with respect to both the number and kinds of ornaments is the influence which led the French to abandon their earlier practice of decorating almost every note, to the detriment of clarity and noble simplicity?

In summary: Good embellishments must be distinguished from bad, the good must be correctly performed, and introduced moderately and fittingly.

. . . Care must be taken to use them sparingly, at the correct places, and without disturbing the affect of a piece. It is understood, for example, that the portrayal of simplicity or sadness suffers fewer ornaments than other emotions. He who observes such principles will be judged perfect, for he will know how to pass skillfully from the singing style to the startling and fiery (in which instruments surpass the voice) and with his constant changing rouse and hold the listener's attention. With these ornaments, the difference between voice and instrument can be unhesitatingly exploited. For the rest, as long as embellishments are applied with discretion no one need pause to decide whether a played passage can or cannot be sung.

Above all things, a prodigal use of embellishments must be avoided. Regard them as spices which may ruin the best dish or gewgaws which may deface the most perfect building. Notes of no great moment and those sufficiently brilliant by themselves should remain free of them, for embellishments serve only to increase the weight and import of notes and to differentiate them from others. Otherwise, I would commit the same error as orators who try to place an impressive accent on every word; everything would be alike and consequently unclear.

THE CLASSICAL ERA

7

Donald Jay Grout

1 9 0 2 -

SOURCES OF CLASSICAL STYLE

IN 1776 DR. CHARLES BURNEY published at London the first
volume of his *General History of Music,* which contains the
following definition: "Music is an innocent luxury, unnecessary,
indeed, to our existence, but a great improvement and gratifi-
cation of the sense of hearing." Less than a hundred years
earlier Andreas Werckmeister had called music "a gift of God,
to be used only in His honor." The contrast between these two
statements illustrates the revolution in thought that had taken
place during the eighteenth century, affecting every department of life.

The complex movement known as "the Enlightenment" began
as a revolt of the spirit: a revolt against supernatural religion
and the church, in favor of natural religion and practical
morality; against metaphysics, in favor of common sense, empirical psychology, applied science, and sociology; against for-
mality, in favor of naturalness; against authority, in favor of
freedom for the individual; and against privilege, in favor of
equal rights and universal education. The temper of the Enlightenment was thus secular, skeptical, empirical, practical,
liberal, equalitarian, and progressive. Its early leaders were
Locke and Hume in England, Montesquieu and Voltaire in
France. The initial phase of the Enlightenment was primarily
negative; but the vacuum left by destructive criticism was soon

51

filled by a new idea: that nature and the natural instincts or feelings of man were the source of true knowledge and right action. Rousseau was the chief apostle of this phase of the Enlightenment, which became conspicuous after about 1760 and which influenced the poet-philosophers Lessing and Herder and the literary movement in Germany described as *Sturm und Drang* (storm and stress).

The two basic ideas of eighteenth-century thought—faith in the efficacy of applied experimental knowledge and faith in the value of common natural feeling—were at one in regarding the individual as both the starting point of investigation and the final criterion of action. Religion, philosophical systems, science, the arts, education, the social order, all were to be judged by how they contributed to the well-being of the individual. "The individual revelling in his own inner life . . . is the characteristic phenomenon of the age of the Enlightenment." The consequences of this viewpoint were evident in many ways, as for example in the ethical systems characteristic of the eighteenth century, which either declared the highest good to be the harmonious development of the innate capacities of the individual, or else, as with the Utilitarians, found the ethical ideal in the formula of "the greatest happiness of the greatest number." The effects of this individualistic bias on the arts, and on music in particular, we shall examine presently.

Life was not guided by the philosophers in the eighteenth century any more than in any other period; systems of thought are responsive to, and influenced by, the conditions of life fully as much as they themselves influence those conditions. Thus, doctrines about the rights of the individual as opposed to the rights of the state, doctrines some of which are incorporated in the American Declaration of Independence and Constitution, grew out of criticism of the terrible inequalities between the common people and the privileged classes. This social criticism was particularly sharp in France in the years before the

Revolution. Advances in the application of scientific discoveries came hand in hand with the beginnings of the industrial revolution; the rise of the philosophy of feeling and the glorification of the natural man (today he would be called the common man) coincided with the rise of the middle class; and so on.

Four aspects of eighteenth-century life and thought are especially important for understanding the music of this period. In the first place, the eighteenth century was a *cosmopolitan* age. National differences were minimized in comparison with the common humanity of men. Foreign-born rulers abounded: German kings in England, Sweden and Poland, a Spanish king in Naples, a French duke in Tuscany, a German princess (Catharine II) as empress of Russia. The Frenchman Voltaire sojourned at the French-speaking court of Frederick the Great of Prussia, and the Italian poet Metastasio at the German imperial court in Vienna; equally typical were the German symphony composers at Paris and the Italian opera composers and singers in Germany, Spain, England, Russia, and France. Quantz, writing at Berlin in 1752, postulates as the ideal musical style one made up of the best features of the music of all nations: "A music that is accepted and recognized as good not by one country only . . . but by many peoples . . . must, provided it is based as well on reason and sound feeling, be beyond all dispute the best." Chabanon, in 1785, declared "Today there is but one music in all of Europe . . . this universal language of our continent." The eighteenth century was receptive to influences from distant ages as well as distant places: the Classical movement took inspiration and example from the art and literature of the ancient world; toward the end of the century, with the beginnings of Romanticism, attention was turned to the Middle Ages, while musicians and poets alike began to take an interest in folk song.

The Enlightenment was *humanitarian* as well as cosmopolitan. Rulers not only patronized arts and letters but also busied themselves with programs of social reform. The eighteenth century was the age of enlightened despots: Frederick the Great of Prussia, Catharine the Great of Russia, Joseph II of Austria, and (in the early part of his reign) Louis XVI of France. Humanitarian ideals, longings for universal human brotherhood, were embodied in the movement of Freemasonry, which spread rapidly over Europe in the eighteenth century and numbered among its adherents kings (Frederick the Great), poets (Goethe), and composers (Mozart). Mozart's *Magic Flute,* Schiller's *Ode to Joy,* and Beethoven's Ninth Symphony were among the outgrowths of the eighteenth-century humanitarian movement.

With the rise of a numerous middle class to a position of influence, the eighteenth century witnessed the first steps in a process of *popularization* of art and learning. A new market was appearing for the productions of writers and artists, and not only the subject matter but also the manner of presentation had to be shaped to the new demands. Philosophy, science, literature, and the fine arts all began to take account of a general public instead of a select group of experts and connoisseurs. Popular treatises were written to bring culture within the reach of all, and novels and plays began to depict everyday people with everyday emotions. Even manners and costumes were affected: at the beginning of the century the bourgeoisie aped the aristocracy; by 1780 the aristocracy aped the lower classes. The popularizing trend found powerful support with the growth of the back to nature movement and the exaltation of sentiment in literature and the arts.

Music was also, of course, affected along with everything else. Patronage was on the wane and the modern musical public was coming into being. Public concerts designed for mixed audiences began to rival the older private concerts and academies: at Paris, a series of public concerts was founded in 1725; another series begun by J. A. Hiller at Leipzig in

1763 was continued after 1781 as the famous *Gewandhaus* concerts; similar concert organizations were founded at Vienna in 1771 and at Berlin in 1790; concert societies had flourished in London sporadically since 1672, and a popular new series began in 1765. Music printing increased enormously; the bulk of the publication was directed at amateurs, and much music was issued in magazines. An amateur public naturally demanded and bought music that was easy to understand and to play, and the same public was interested in reading about and discussing music. Musical journalism began; after the middle of the century magazines sprang up which were devoted to musical news, reviews, and criticism. The first histories of music were written and the first collection of medieval musical treatises published.

Finally, the Enlightenment was a *prosaic* age. Its best literature was prose, and it valued in all the arts the virtues of good prose writing: clarity, animation, good taste, proportion, and elegance. Rational rather than poetic, the age had little liking for Baroque mysticism, gravity, massiveness, grandeur, and passion, and its critical temper inhibited great poetry in large forms. Early eighteenth-century aesthetics held that the task of music, like that of the other arts, was to imitate nature, to offer to the listener pleasant sounding images of reality. Music was supposed to imitate not the actual sounds of the world of nature, but rather the sounds of speech, especially as these expressed the sentiments of the soul; according to Rousseau and some others, it should imitate a mythical primitive speech-song, assumed to be the natural language of man; or again, music might in some way imitate the feelings themselves, not necessarily by imitating speech. Only toward the end of the century did theorists gradually come to think that music might move the feelings directly through the beauty of sounds and that a work of music might develop in accordance with its own nature, independent of any model. But even then the idea of imitation persisted; music was an imitative, hence a decorative art, "an innocent luxury," as Dr. Burney called it.

Moreover, music of the Enlightenment was supposed to meet the listener on his own ground, and not compel him to make an anxious effort to understand what was going on; it must please (by agreeable sounds and rational structure) and move (by imitating feelings) , but not too often astonish (by excessive elaboration) and never puzzle (by too great complexity). Music, as "the art of pleasing by the succession and combination of agreeable sounds" must eschew contrapuntal complexities, which could only be appreciated by the few learned in such abstruse matters. Not all writers went so far in this respect as Rousseau, who defined musical composition as "the art of inventing tunes and accompanying them with suitable harmonies" and declared that "to sing two melodies at once is like making two speeches at once in order to be more forceful" but Quantz felt that "the old composers were too much absorbed with musical 'tricks' [contrapuntal devices] and carried them too far, so that they neglected the essential thing in music, which is to move and please." Burney criticised J. S. Bach as having in his organ works "been constantly in search of what was new and difficult, without the least attention to nature and facility" and regretted that that master could not have learned to sacrifice "all unmeaning art and contrivance" in his compositions and write "in a style more popular, and generally intelligible and pleasing." It is only fair to mention that Burney later achieved a better understanding of Bach's music; but the opinions expressed above were shared by most critics in the 1780's, and the expressive qualities of eighteenth-century music are often sentimental and childlike, bound up as they are with this constant striving for naturalness and simplicity.

The ideal music in the eighteenth century, then, might be described as follows: its language should be universal, not limited by national boundaries; it should be noble as well as entertaining; it should be expressive within the bounds of decorum; it should be natural, that is, free of needless technical complications and capable of immediately pleasing any normally sensitive listener. The music that most nearly realized these ideals was written in the Classical period, approximately the years 1770 to 1800, and its masters were Gluck, Haydn, Mozart, and the young Beethoven.

This formula is not advanced as an explanation of all eighteenth-century music, but only as a summary of the general aims which seem to have more or less consciously governed the minds of both composers and audiences, particularly in the last thirty years of the century. No formula could possibly comprehend the manifold aspects of all the music composed between 1700 and 1800. The Baroque yielded only gradually to new styles, and the old and the new existed side by side. . . . Yet after about 1740 the change of style was generally noticeable.

The eighteenth-century was a cosmopolitan age; nonetheless, lively arguments about the relative merits of various national musical styles were carried on up to the eve of the French Revolution; moreover, after 1750 in every country new national forms of opera were coming to the fore, harbingers of the Romantic era. The eighteenth-century stream of humanitarian idealism did not markedly affect music until the time of the French Revolution, and may even be considered, like the rise of national opera and the growth of interest in folk song, as a pre-Romantic trait.

Because Gluck, and more especially Haydn and Mozart, overshadow their predecessors and contemporaries in much the same way that Bach and Handel overshadow theirs, it is easy to fall into the error of viewing the late seventeenth-century composers merely as the forerunners of Bach and Handel, and the mid-eighteenth century composers merely as the forerunners of Gluck, Haydn, and Mozart. It is especially easy in the latter instance because so little is yet known about either eighteeenth-century opera or the origins of the Classical symphony. This area is one of the comparatively blank spots in music history, and until more information about it is available any endeavor to deal with it in a comprehensive way must be regarded as tentative. The fallacy of this "mere forerunner" conception is undoubtedly due to a confused notion that progress occurs when old things are superseded by new; we are prone to imagine that in the same way that the automobile superseded the horse and buggy, the symphonies of Mozart superseded those of Stamitz. To deny this is not to deny that Mozart was a greater composer than Stamitz, but only to assert that the idea of progress is not necessarily relevant in comparing the two. . . .

Two general styles or manners can be distinguished within the so-called pre-Classical period beginning around 1720: the *rococo* and the *expressive*. The former was cultivated especially in France, and the French term *style galant* (gallant style) is often used as a synonym for rococo. The expressive style, which arose somewhat later and was chiefly associated with German composers, is often designated by the equivalent German phrase *empfindsamer Stil* (literally, "sensitive" style). Both may be regarded as outgrowths of the Baroque tendency to concentrate all musical interest in the two outer voices; but in these newer styles the bass loses all vestiges of leadership and contrapuntal independence, and becomes merely a background for the melody, while the inner voices hardly exist at all.

The rococo or gallant style arose in courtly, aristocratic circles; it was elegant, playful, easy, witty, polished, and ornate. *Rococo* originally described the elaborately ornamental decoration of interiors and furnishings fashionable in France during the age of the Regency; *galant* was a catch word of the same period, applied to everything that was thought to be modern, smart, chic, smooth, easy, and sophisticated. The rococo is Baroque decorativeness without grandeur. The expressive style, on the other hand, was an affair of the middle class; it was the *style bourgeois*. Instead of being ornate, it is sometimes ostentatiously plain. It domesticates the Baroque affections, turning them into sentiments of the individual soul. The ease and elegance of the rococo, as well as some of its decorative charm, were combined with the expressive quality of the *style bourgeois* in most compositions by the middle of the eightenth century, and both styles are completely absorbed into the music of the Classical period.

The change from Baroque to the new kind of eighteeenth-century music included among other things a change in the conception of melody and melodic development. The normal Baroque technique had been to announce the theme of a movement—the melodic-rhythmic subject embodying the basic affection—at the outset; this material was then spun out, with relatively infrequent and usually inconspicuous cadences, and with sequential repetition of phrases as the principal articulating device within periods. The result was a highly integrated movement without sharp contrasts, or else (as in the Vivaldi concertos) a formal pattern of contrasts between thematic tutti and nonthematic solo sections; but in either case the phrase structure was usually so irregular and complex that there was no marked feeling of periodicity, of antecedent-and-consequent phrases. The new composers of the eighteenth century, while retaining the late Baroque method of constructing a movement on the basis of related keys, gradually abandoned the older idea of the one basic affection and began to introduce contrasts between the various parts of a movement or even within the theme or themes themselves. Moreover, instead of the Baroque spinning-out technique and complex phraseology, the melodies were organized into more distinct phrases of regular two- or four-bar lengths, resulting in a periodic structure. . . . All melodies, but especially slow ones, kept a certain amount of ornamentation; as C. P. E. Bach wrote in 1753, "Probably no one has ever doubted the necessity of embellishments." The graceful, lyric charm which we ordinarly call "Mozartean" is not peculiar to Mozart, but is part of the common musical language of the second half of the century.

The harmonic vocabulary and tonal system of the middle and late eighteenth century were substantially the same as those of the late Baroque, but the harmonic rhythm of most of the new music is slower and the harmonic progressions less weighty than in the older style. A great deal of bustling melodic activity goes on over relatively slow-moving and conventional harmonies, and important harmonic changes almost always coincide with the strong accents indicated by the barlines.

8

David Boyden

1910-

CLASSICAL STYLE

David Boyden is a musicologist who teaches at the University of California in Berkeley. In addition to studies of eighteenth-century music, his published works include *An Introduction to Music* (1956), from which the excerpts included here were taken.

THE CLASSICISM of the late eighteenth century was actually influenced by the study of Classical antiquity. But the term "Classic," used originally in literature, dates from the early nineteenth century. It was used by the Romantic movement to differentiate its art of freedom and inspiration from the art of established rules of the eighteenth century. . . .

In music, the rococo style originated in a reaction against counterpoint and the comparatively austere style of earlier composers like Bach and Handel. The sons of J. S. Bach thought their father's music was old-fashioned, although they greatly respected it. Rousseau thought counterpoint was as absurd as several people talking at once; to him Pergolesi's simple, catchy tunes and transparent harmonies were the ideal. In spite of this attitude, counterpoint ("the learned" style) persisted in certain types of music, notably church music. The new fashion encouraged a vogue of harmony and melody that was simplicity itself. Compared to the long arch of melody that had been characteristic of Bach, the "new" melody was short-breathed and repetitive. Typical were short phrases of two or four measures balanced against each other either by repetition or by contrast of different short melodies.

The rococo melodies were basically ornamental and expressive in character. Just as works of art were decorated with rockwork and shells, the music was elaborated by musical ornamentation . . . In contrast to this rather sentimental lyricism, there was also a type of bold and robust passage work, almost, it would seem, inspired by the spirit of the *Sturm und Drang*, and based on scale passages and broken chords. A number of composers combined the lyric and robust style, among them C.P.E. Bach, most characteristically, and in their early works, Gluck, Haydn, and Mozart. A special type of melody, *the singing allegro*, was typical of J. C. (the "London") Bach, and after him, of Mozart. In *the singing allegro*, a songlike element was introduced into a fast movement by setting a lyrical theme to notes of comparatively long duration in an otherwise rapid movement. These elements were all amalgamated in the Classic style of Haydn and Mozart. In them the same general attitude toward balanced and contrasted phrase structure prevailed, but their mature works exhibit a kind of melody purified of the excess of extravagant decoration, empty scale passages, and sentimentality.

With the chief interest concentrated in the melody, the other voices were often pushed into the background merely as accompaniment. This was especially true of the rococo of the early Classic period. In order to enliven the harmonic support, composers resorted to various devices. Among these was the *Alberti bass* (so called after the composer, Alberti), in which the chords of the harmony were broken up into figures and rhythmically animated . . .

One of the chief problems of the new style was to replace the old figured bass with an appropriate substitute. . . . After 1750, the figured bass was gradually rendered obsolete by the new style, and the basic harmonies had to be supplied in other ways. On the harpsichord, for example, the melody was assigned to the right hand and the harmonies to the left. To animate them the Alberti bass was frequently used. In the orchestra, the fundamental harmonies were delegated to certain groups of instruments, notably the brasses and woodwinds; in fact, the whole orchestra became more clearly divided into melodic and harmonic instruments. However, a texture or style of orchestration that assigned all the melodic interest to one part or to one type of instrument and relegated the subordinate harmonies to the rest was inherently limited in perspective and monotonous to the audience and to the player. This impoverished harmonic style was characteristic of the rococo, and it presented a serious problem for composers. Somehow the texture had to be enriched harmonically and enlivened rhythmically. Haydn was the first to see how this could be done (in the String Quartets of Op. 33, 1783). In effect he retained the chordal harmony of his time but permeated this harmonic texture with melodic motives derived from the principal melodies. Thus the texture ceased to be merely a dominant melody supported by subordinate chords. All the voice parts shared in the melodic interest, at least periodically, because snatches of melody in the form of motives were assigned to various voices in turn. Haydn had really imposed a kind of motivic polyphony on a melodic-harmonic texture, and he had solved the problem of monotony inherent in pure harmony. . . .

To gain greater contrast and increased expressiveness, the composers of the whole Classic period used a wider gradation of dynamics (louds and softs) than was used previously. Furthermore, their attitude toward dynamics was somewhat different from that of their predecessors. With Bach and Handel, the *crescendo* and *diminuendo* was usually limited to single notes or parts of measures. Classic composers began to use a *continuous crescendo* that lasted several measures or more—a device exploited first by the celebrated orchestra at the Mannheim court under J.W.A. Stamitz (1717-57). Other dynamic effects that characterized the new style were the *sforzando* (a sudden forcing of tone) and sudden contrasts of the extremes of loud and soft.

To meet the requirements of a new style, changes in the instruments occurred. The typical keyboard instruments that remained from the preceding period were adapted to the new conditions or they yielded to new substitutes. The organ, for example, was made capable of producing *crescendo* and *diminuendo* by means of the so-called Venetian shutter; and the harpsichord, which is incapable of any appreciable graduation between louds and softs, gradually became obsolete, yielding its place to the pianoforte. The latter could produce a great range of *crescendo* and *diminuendo* as well as the smallest nuance of tone, and its gradations of tone and color were admirably suited to an expressive and personal style of music and performance. Although an instrument of ancient origin, the clavichord, with its possibility of nuance, expression, and bell-like tone, was in some respects the ideal instrument of the rococo. But the dynamic range of the clavichord was so small that for all practical purposes the pianoforte became the principal keyboard instrument outside the church. However, the pianoforte of Mozart's time was quite different from the pianoforte today. The tone was weaker and also clearer, particularly in the bass. The tension of the strings was far less, and the frame was much less reinforced. As compared with the modern pianoforte, the tone of the instrument of Mozart's time resembled that of the stringed instruments more closely and blended with them much better.

In the orchestra new instruments were added. The clarinet, for example, proved a valuable addition because of its wide range and the contrasted tone colors of different parts of its register. More important than the introduction of single new instruments was the change in the way all the instruments were used, that is, in orchestration. The modern divisions of the orchestra and their function were established at this time. A clear division was made between the instruments that were to play melodic passages and those which were to sustain the harmonies. The different instruments of the orchestra were more clearly divided into choirs of like instruments: the strings, woodwinds, brasses, and percussion. The Mannheim orchestra, one of the most progressive of the day, standardized the arrangement at about fifty players (the modern symphony orchestra has about a hundred) , and the following subdivisions:

(1) the *strings:* violin I, violin II, viola, cello bass (the cello and the bass used the same written part until Beethoven's time, but the bass sounded an octave below the cello) .

(2) the *woodwinds:* oboe (and/or clarinet) I and II, flute I and II, bassoon I and II.

(3) the *brasses:* horn I and II, trumpet I and II.

(4) the *percussion:* timpani (kettledrums) tuned to the tonic and the dominant.

Generally speaking, the higher strings and the woodwinds were used melodically, and as occasion demanded, harmonically. The other instruments were used harmonically, or sometimes for special effects, such as fanfare figures played by the trumpets. The woodwinds and the brasses were used more to hold harmony notes than to play melodies because of the limited number of notes at their disposal.

9

Aaron Copland

1900-

SONATA FORM

*The American composer, Aaron Copland, has also written ex-
tensively about music. "Sonata form" is an extract from What to
Listen for in Music, first published in 1939.*

THE SONATA FORM, for the present-day listener, has something
of the same significance that the fugal forms had for listeners
of the first part of the eighteenth century. For it is not too
much to say that, since that time, the basic form of almost
every extended piece of music has been related in some way to
the sonata. The vitality of the form is astonishing. It is just as
much alive today as it was during the period of its first development. The logic of the form as it was practiced in the early
days, plus its malleability in the hands of later composers,
accounts, no doubt, for its continuous hold on the imagination of musical creators for the past 150 years or more.

Of course, it must not be forgotten that when we speak of
sonata form we are not discussing only the form to be found in
pieces that are called sonatas, for the meaning of the term is
much more widespread than that. Every symphony, for example, is a sonata for orchestra; every string quartet is a sonata
for four strings; every concerto a sonata for a solo instrument and orchestra. Most overtures, also, are in the form of
the first movement of a sonata. The usage of the term sonata

itself is generally confined to compositions for a solo instrument, with or without piano accompaniment; but, as may easily be seen, that is not nearly broad enough to include the varied applications of what is, in fact, sonata form to different mediums. . . .

The sonata as we think of it is said to be largely the creation of one of Bach's sons, Karl Philipp Emanuel Bach. He is credited with having been one of the first composers to experiment with the new form of sonata, the classic outlines of which were later definitely set by Haydn and Mozart. Beethoven put all his genius into broadening the sonata-form conceptions of his time; and he was followed by Schumann and Brahms, who also extended, in a lesser way, the significance of the formal mold. By now the treatment of the form is so free as to be almost unrecognizable in certain cases. Nevertheless, much of the outer shell and a good deal of the psychological implications of the form are intact, even today.

The Sonata as a Whole

Three or four separate movements comprise the sonata as a whole. There are examples of two-movement and, more recently, one-movement sonatas, but these are exceptional. The most obvious distinction between the movements is one of tempo: in the three-movement species, it is fast—slow—fast; and in the four-movement sonata, it is usually fast—slow—moderately fast—very fast.

People generally want to know what it is that makes these three or four movements belong together. No one has come forward with a completely satisfactory answer to that question. Custom and familiarity make them *seem* to belong together, but I have always suspected that one could substitute the Minuet of Haydn's 98th symphony for the Minuet in Haydn's

99th symphony without sensing a serious lack of coherence in either work. Particularly in these early examples of the sonata, the movements are linked together more from the need of balance and contrast and certain tonality relationships than from any intrinsic connection with each other. Later on, as we shall see in the so-called cyclic form of the sonata, composers did try to link their movements through thematic unity while retaining the general characteristics of the separate movements.

Now let us consider, for a moment, the form of each of the separate movements of the sonata as a whole. Our descriptions are to be taken as generally true, for there is almost no statement that can be made about sonata form that some specific exceptional instance does not contradict. . . . The first movement of any sonata—and I use that word generically to denote symphonies and string quartets and the like—is always in sonata-allegro form. We shall be investigating that form thoroughly a few pages farther on.

The second movement is usually the slow movement, but there is no such thing as a slow-movement form. It may be written in one of several different molds. For example, it may be a theme and variation . . . or it may be a slow version of a rondo form—either a short or an extended rondo. It might be even more simple than that, relating itself to the ordinary three-part sectional form. More rarely, it bears close resemblance to the first-movement sonata form. The listener must be prepared for any one of these various forms when hearing the slow movement.

The third movement is usually a minuet or scherzo. In the earlier works of Haydn and Mozart, it is the minuet; in later times, the scherzo. In either case, it is *A-B-A,* three-part form. . . . Sometimes the second and third movements are interchangeable—instead of finding the slow movement second and the scherzo third, the scherzo may be second and the slow movement third.

The fourth movement, or finale, as it is often called, is almost always either in extended rondo form or in sonata-allegro form. Thus it is only the first movement of the sonata that presents an entirely new physiognomy for us. . . .

The conventional explanation of sonata-allegro form is easily demonstrated. It explains, for the most part, the earlier and less complex forms of the sonata allegro. A simple diagram will show the general outlines of the form:

	Exposition			Development	Recapitulation	
|	A	: ||		B	A	|
| a |	b |	c |	|	a b c |	| a | b | c |	
tonic	dominant	dominant		foreign keys	tonic tonic tonic	

As may be seen, the *A-B-A* of the formula is, in this instance, named exposition-development-recapitulation. In the exposition section, the thematic material is exposed; in the development section, it is handled in new and unsuspected ways; in the recapitulation, it is heard again in its original setting. . . .

So much for the bare outlines of the form. Now let us examine it more closely and see if we cannot generalize regarding the form in such a way as to make it more applicable to actual examples of all periods.

All sonata allegros, of whatever period, retain the tripartite form of exposition-development-recapitulation. The exposition contains a variety of musical elements. That is its essential nature, for there would be little or nothing to develop if that were not so. These varied elements are usually divided into a small *a*, a small *b,* and a small *c*, representing what used to be called the first, second, and closing themes. I say "used to be called" because recent analysts have become dissatisfied with the obvious disparity between this nomenclature and the evidence presented by the actual works themselves. It is difficult to generalize with any degree of finality as to exactly what goes into an exposition section. Still, one can safely say that themes *are* exposed, that these themes are contrasted in character, and that they bring some sense of close at the end of the section. For the sake of convenience, there would be no objection to calling the small *a* the first theme, provided it were clearly understood that actually it may consist of a conglomeration of several themes or fragments of themes, usually of a strongly dramatic and affirmative quality. The same is true of the *b*, so-called second, theme, which again may actually be a series of one or more themes, but of a more lyrical and expressive nature. This juxtaposition of one group of themes denoting power and aggressiveness with another group which is relaxed and more songlike in quality is the essence of the exposition section and determines the character of the entire sonata-allegro form. In many of the early examples of the form, the ordering of the material into first and second themes is more strictly adhered to, whereas later on we can be sure only that two opposing elements will be present in the exposition, without being able to say in exactly what sequence they will appear.

The last theme, or themes, under the heading of small *c*, constitutes a closing sentence or sentences. Therefore it may be of any nature that leads to a sense of conclusion. This is important, because an audience should have a clear idea of where the end of the exposition occurs, if it is expected to follow the development intelligently. If you read notes, you can always mechanically find the end of the exposition in any of the classic sonatas or symphonies by looking for the double bar with repeat sign, indicating the formal repetition of the entire section. Interpreters nowadays use their discretion in the matter of repeating the exposition. So that part of the problem of listening to the first-movement form is to watch out for this possibility of repetition. More modern sonatas and symphonies do not indicate any repetition, so that even if you read notes the end of the section is not so easily found.

One other element is important in the exposition. You cannot very well go from one mood that is powerfully dramatic to another that is lyrically expressive without some sort of transition. This transition, or bridge section, as it is often called, may be short or fairly elaborate. But it must never be of equal significance thematically with elements *a* or *b,* for that could lead only to confusion. Composers, at such moments, fall back upon a kind of musical figuration, or passage work, which is important because of its functional significance rather than for its intrinsic musical interest. Watch out, then, for the bridge between *a* and *b* and the possibility of a second bridge between *b* and *c.*

It is the development section that gives the sonata allegro its special character. In no other form is there a special division reserved for the extension and development of musical material already introduced in a previous section. It is that feature of the sonata-allegro form that has so fascinated all composers— that opportunity for working freely with materials already announced. So you see that the sonata form, properly understood, is essentially a psychological and dramatic form. You cannot very well mix the two or more elements of the exposition without creating a sense of struggle or drama. It is the development section that challenges the imagination of every composer. One might go so far as to say that it is one of the main things that separates the composer from the layman. For anyone can whistle tunes. But you really have to be a composer, with a composer's craft and technique, in order to be able to write a really fine development of those tunes.

No rules govern the development section. The composer is entirely free as to types of development, as to the thematic material chosen for development; as to the introduction of new materials, if any; and as to the length of the section as a whole.

One can only generalize about two factors: (1) that the development usually begins with a partial restatement of the first theme in order to remind the listener of the starting point; and (2) that during the course of the development the music modulates through a series of far-off keys which serve to prepare a sense of homecoming when the original tonality is finally reached at the beginning of the recapitulation. These things vary considerably, of course, in accordance with whether you examine an early or late example of sonata-allegro form. For instance, the development section became much more elaborate, even as early as Beethoven's day, than it had been before his time. The modulatory scheme has been adhered to, even in recent times, when the classic tonic-dominant-dominant relationship of the first, second, and closing themes, respectively, has completely broken down. More and more the trend has been to attach added importance to the development section, as I have already pointed out, so that it has become the pivotal section of the sonata-allegro form, into which the composer pours every ounce of imagination and invention that he possesses.

The recapitulation is, as its name indicates, a repetition of the exposition. In the classical sonata-allegro, the repetition is generally exact; though even here the inclination is to omit nonessentials, leaving out material already sufficiently heard. In later times, the repetition became more and more free until it sometimes is a mere wraith of its former self. It is not very difficult to understand why this is so. The sonata-allegro had its origin in a period when composers were "classically" minded; that is, they began with a structure whose outlines were perfectly clear, and into it they put a music well controlled and of an objective emotional quality. There was no contradiction between the formal *A-B-A* outline and the nature of the musical content. But with the advent of the Romantic era, music became much more dramatic and psychological. It was inevitable that the new romantic content should be difficult to contain within the framework of an essentially classical formal scheme. For it is only logical to say that if the composer states his material in the exposition, and if he then develops it in a highly dramatic and psychological fashion, he really should come to a different conclusion about it in the end. What sense does it make to go through all the turmoil and struggle of the development section if it is only to lead back to the same conclusions from which we started? That is why the tendency on the part of modern composers to shorten the recapitulation or to substitute a new conclusion seems justified . . .

Two important extensions were added to the form while it was still in the early stages of development. An introductory section preceded the "allegro," and a coda was tacked on at the end. The introduction is almost always slow in tempo, a sure indication that the A section has not yet begun. It may consist of musical materials which are entirely independent of the allegro to follow; or it may be that a slow version of the main theme in A is given out to further the feeling of unity. The coda cannot be so definitely described. From Beethoven on, it has played a preponderant role in stretching the boundaries of the form. Its purpose is to create a sense of apotheosis—the material is seen for the last time and in a new light. Here, again, no rules govern the procedure. At times, the treatment is so extended as to make the coda a kind of second development section though always leading toward a sense of epilogue and conclusion. . . .

The Symphony

The present-day status of the symphony is such that it is impossible to pass it by without further discussion, even though it does not constitute an independent form, different from the sonata. It is practically impossible to hear an orchestral program in the concert hall or on the air without being confronted with one or another of the symphonies of the regular repertoire. It should be remembered, however, that these present no specific problems other than those outlined above.

The symphony had its origin not in instrumental forms like the concerto grosso, as one might have expected, but in the overture of early Italian opera. The overture, or sinfornia, as it was called, as perfected by Alessandro Scarlatti consisted of three parts: fast-slow-fast, thus presaging the three movements of the classical symphony. The sinfornia, around 1750, became detached from the opera which gave it birth and led an independent life in the concert hall. . . .

The best orchestra of the day was maintained from 1743 to 1777 in Mannheim. Here the precursors of Haydn and Mozart originated many of the features of the later symphony, such as the orchestral crescendo and diminuendo and a greater flexibility in the orchestral fabric. The general texture was more homophonic, borrowing from the lighter, singing quality of operatic style, rather than the heavier contrapuntal manner of the concerto grosso.

It was on this foundation that Haydn gradually perfected symphonic style. We must not forget that some of his greatest achievements in this medium were created after the death of Mozart and after a long period of gestation and maturity. He left the symphony a rounded art form, capable of further development but not of greater perfection within the limits of his own style.

The way was paved for Beethoven's famous Nine. The symphony lost all connection with its operatic origins. The form was enlarged, the emotional scope broadened, the orchestra stamped and thundered in a completely new and unheard-of fashion. Beethoven singlehandedly created a colossus which he alone seemed able to control.

For the nineteenth-century composers who followed him—Schumann and Mendelssohn—wrote a less titanic symphony. By the middle of the century, the symphony was in danger of losing its hegemony in the orchestral field. The "modernists" Liszt, Berlioz, and Wagner apparently considered the symphony "old hat" unless it was combined with some programmatic idea or incorporated in essence into the body of a music drama. It was "conservatives" like Brahms, Bruckner, and Tschaikovsky who defended what began to look very much like a lost cause.

One important innovation was introduced during this period as regards symphonic form, namely, the so-called cyclic form of the symphony. César Franck was especially fond of this device. It was an attempt to bind the different parts of the entire work by unifying the thematic materials. Sometimes a "motto" theme is heard at unexpected moments in different movements of the symphony, giving an impression of a single unifying thought. At other times—and this is more truly cyclic form—all thematic material in an entire symphony may be derived from only a few primal themes, which are completely metamorphosized as the work progresses, so that what was first given out as a sober introductory theme is transformed into the principal melody of the scherzo, and similarly in slow movement and finale.

If the cyclic form has not been adopted more widely, it is probably because it does not solve the need for musical logic within each separate movement. That is, the unification of all the thematic material is no more than a device, more or less interesting depending upon the ingenuity with which it is carried out by the composer, but the symphony itself must still be written! The same problems of form and substance must be grappled with, compared to which the derivation of all the material from a single source is only a detail.

10

Christoph Willibald Gluck

1714-1787

DEDICATION FROM *ALCESTE*

Opera in the early eighteenth century had become chiefly a vehicle for displaying the vocal prowess of "star" singers. Gluck attempted to reestablish a balance and interrelationship between the music and the drama in a number of operas written in a new style emphasizing dramatic expression. *Alceste* was first performed in Vienna, December 16, 1767.

YOUR ROYAL HIGHNESS:

When I undertook to write the music for *Alceste,* I resolved to divest it entirely of all those abuses, introduced into it either by the mistaken vanity of singers or by the too great complaisance of composers. which have so long disfigured Italian opera and made of the most splendid and most beautiful of spectacles the most ridiculous and wearisome. I have striven to restrict music to its true office of serving poetry by means of expression and by following the situations of the story, without interrupting the action or stifling it with a useless superfluity of ornaments; and I believed that it should do this in the same way as telling colors affect a correct and well-ordered drawing, by a well-assorted contrast of light and shade, which serves to animate the figures without altering their contours. Thus I did not wish to arrest an actor in the greatest heat of dialogue in order to wait for a tiresome *ritornello,* nor to hold him up in the middle of a word on a vowel favorable to his voice, nor to make display of the agility of his fine voice in some long-drawn passage, nor to wait while the orchestra gives him time to recover his breath for a cadenza. I did not think it my duty to pass quickly over the second section[1] of an aria of which the words are perhaps the most impassioned and important, in order to repeat regularly four times over those of the first part, and to finish the aria where its sense may perhaps not end for the convenience of the singer who wishes to show that he can capriciously vary a passage in a number of guises; in short, I have sought to abolish all the abuses against which good sense and reason have long cried out in vain.

I have felt that the overture ought to apprise the spectators of the nature of the action that is to be represented and to form, so to speak, its argument; that the concerted instruments should be introduced in proportion to the interest and the intensity of the words, and not leave that sharp contrast between the aria and the recitative in the dialogue, so as not to break a period unreasonably nor wantonly disturb the force and heat of the action.

Furthermore, I believed that my greatest labor should be devoted to seeking a beautiful simplicity, and I have avoided making displays of difficulty at the expense of clearness; nor did I judge it desirable to discover novelties if it was not naturally suggested by the situation and the expression; and there is no rule which I have not thought it right to set aside willingly for the sake of an intended effect.

Such are my principles. By good fortune my designs were wonderfully furthered by the libretto, in which the celebrated

[1] By "second section" Gluck means the central or contrasting section of the da capo aria. In the eighteenth century the first section of such an aria regularly presented its full text twice and had then to be repeated after the central or contrasting section, hence Gluck's reference to repeating the words of the first part "four times over."

author, devising a new dramatic scheme, for florid descriptions, unnatural paragons, and sententious, cold morality, had substituted heartfelt language, strong passions, interesting situations and an endlessly varied spectacle. The success of the work justified my maxims, and the universal approbation of so enlightened a city has made it clearly evident that simplicity, truth and naturalness are the great principles of beauty in all artistic manifestations. For all that, in spite of repeated urgings on the part of some most eminent persons to decide upon the publication of this opera of mine in print, I was well aware of all the risk run in combating such firmly and profoundly rooted prejudices, and I thus felt the necessity of fortifying myself with the most powerful patronage of YOUR ROYAL HIGHNESS, whose August Name I beg you may have the grace to prefix to this my opera, a name which with so much justice enjoys the suffrages of an enlightened Europe. The great protector of the fine arts, who reigns over a nation that had the glory of making them arise again from universal oppression and which itself has produced the greatest models, in a city that was always the first to shake off the yoke of vulgar prejudices in order to clear a path for perfection, may alone undertake the reform of that noble spectacle in which all the fine arts take so great a share. If this should succeed, the glory of having moved the first stone will remain for me, and in this public testimonial of Your Highness's furtherance of the same, I have the honor to subscribe myself, with the most humble respect.

Your Royal Highness's
    Most humble, most devoted, and most obliged servant,

CHRISTOFORO GLUCK

11

Wolfgang Amadeus Mozart

1756-1791

ON COMPOSING AN OPERA:
THE ABDUCTION FROM THE SERAGLIO

The *Abduction from the Seraglio* is a comic opera begun
by Mozart in July 1781, completed in June of the following
year, and first performed on July 16, 1782. The libretto was
written by Gottlieb Stephanie.

Vienne, ce 26 *de Septembre,* 1781

MON TRES CHER PERE!

Forgive me for having made you pay an extra heavy postage
fee the other day. But I happened to have nothing important
to tell you and thought that it would afford you pleasure if I
gave you some idea of my opera. As the original text began
with a monologue, I asked Herr Stephanie to make a little
arietta out of it—and then to put in a duet instead of making
the two chatter together after Osmin's short song. As we have
given the part of Osmin to Herr Fischer, who certainly has
an excellent bass voice (in spite of the fact that the Archbishop
told me that he sang too low for a bass and that I assured
him that he would sing higher next time), we must take advantage of it, particularly as he has the whole Viennese public
on his side. But in the original libretto Osmin has only this
short song and nothing else to sing, except in the trio and the
finale; so he has been given an aria in Act I, and he is to have

another in Act II. I have explained to Stephanie the words I require for this aria—indeed I had finished composing most of the music for it before Stephanie knew anything whatever about it. I am enclosing only the beginning and the end, which is bound to have a good effect. Osmin's rage is rendered comical by the accompaniment of the Turkish music. In working out the aria I have given full scope now and then to Fischer's beautiful deep notes (in spite of our Salzburg Midas). The passage "Drum beim Barte des Propheten" is indeed in the same tempo, but with quick notes; but as Osmin's rage gradually increases, there comes (just when the aria seems to be at an end) the allegro assai, which is in a totally different measure and in a different key; this is bound to be very effective. For just as a man in such a towering rage oversteps all the bounds of order, moderation and propriety and completely forgets himself, so must the music too forget itself. But as passions, whether violent or not, must never be expressed in such a way as to excite disgust, and as music, even in the most terrible situations, must never offend the ear, but must please the hearer, or in other words must never cease to be *music,* I have gone from F (the key in which the aria is written), not into a remote key, but into a related one, not, however, into its nearest relative D minor, but into the more remote A minor. Let me now turn to Belmonte's aria in A major, "O wie ängstlich, o wie feurig." Would you like to know how I have expressed it—and even indicated his throbbing heart? By the two violins playing octaves. This is the favourite aria of all those who have heard it, and it is mine also. I wrote it expressly to suit Adamberger's voice. You feel the trembling—the faltering—you see how his throbbing breast begins to swell; this I have expressed by a crescendo. You hear the whispering and the sighing—which I have indicated by the first violins with mutes and a flute playing in unison.

The Janissary chorus is, as such, all that can be desired, that is, short, lively and written to please the Viennese. I have sacrificed Constanze's aria a little to the flexible throat of Mlle Cavalieri, "Trennung war mein banges Los und nun schwimmt mein Aug' in Tränen." I have tried to express her feelings, as far as an Italian bravura aria will allow it. I have changed the "Hui" to "schnell," so it now runs thus—"Doch wie schnell schwand meine Freude." I really don't know what our German poets are thinking of. Even if they do not understand the theatre, or at all events operas, yet they should not make their characters talk as if they were addressing a herd of swine. Hui, sow!

Now for the trio at the close of Act. I. Pedrillo has passed off his master as an architect—to give him an opportunity of meeting his Constanze in the garden. Bassa Selim has taken him into his service. Osmin, the steward, knows nothing of this, and being a rude churl and a sworn foe to all strangers, is impertinent and refuses to let them into the garden. It opens quite abruptly—and because the words lend themselves to it, I have made it a fairly respectable piece of real three-part writing. Then the major key begins at once pianissimo—it must go very quickly—and wind up with a great deal of noise, which is always appropriate at the end of an act. The more noise the better, and the shorter the better, so that the audience may not have time to cool down with their applause.

I have sent you only fourteen bars of the ouverture, which is very short with alternate fortes and pianos, the Turkish music always coming in at the fortes. The ouverture modulates through different keys; and I doubt whether anyone, even if his previous night has been a sleepless one, could go to sleep over it. Now comes the rub! The first act was finished more than three weeks ago, as was also one aria in Act II and the drunken duet (*per i signori viennesi*) which consists entirely of *my Turkish tattoo.* But I cannot compose any more, because the whole story is being altered—and, to tell the truth, at my own request. At the beginning of Act III there is a charming quintet or rather finale, but I should prefer to have it at the end of Act II. In order to make this practicable, great changes must be made, in fact an entirely new plot must be introduced—and Stephanie is up to the eyes in other work. So we must have a little patience. Everyone abuses Stephanie. It may be that in my case he is only very friendly to my face. But after all he is arranging the libretto for me—and, what is more, as I want it—exactly—and, by Heaven, I do not ask anything more of him. Well, how I have been chattering to you about my opera! But I cannot help it. . . .

your most obedient son

W. A. Mozart

Vienne, ce 13 *d'octobre,* 1781

Mon tres cher pere!

. . . Now as to the libretto of the opera. You are quite right so far as Stephanie's work is concerned. Still, the poetry is perfectly in keeping with the character of stupid, surly, malicious Osmin. I am well aware that the verse is not of the best, but it fitted in and it agreed so well with the musical ideas which already were buzzing in my head, that it could not fail to please me; and I would like to wager that when it is performed, no deficiencies will be found. As for the poetry which was there originally, I really have nothing to say against it. Belmonte's aria "O wie ängstlich" could hardly be better written for music. Except for "Hui" and "Kummer ruht in meinem Schoss" (for sorrow—cannot rest), the aria too is not bad, particularly the first part. Besides, I should say that in an opera the poetry must be altogether the obedient daughter of the music. Why do Italian comic operas please everywhere—in spite of their mis-

82

erable libretti—even in Paris, where I myself witnessed their success? Just because there the music reigns supreme and when one listens to it all else is forgotten. Why, an opera is sure of success when the plot is well worked out, the words written solely for the music and not shoved in here and there to suit some miserable rhyme (which, God knows, never enhances the value of any theatrical performance, be it what it may, but rather detracts from it) —I mean, words or even entire verses which ruin the composer's whole idea. Verses are indeed the most indispensable element for music—but rhymes—solely for the sake of rhyming—the most detrimental. Those high and mighty people who set to work in this pedantic fashion will always come to grief, both they and their music. The best thing of all is when a good composer, who understands the stage and is talented enough to make sound suggestions, meets an able poet, that true phoenix; in that case no fears need be entertained as to the applause even of the ignorant. Poets almost remind me of trumpeters with their professional tricks! If we composers were always to stick so faithfully to our rules (which were very good at a time when no one knew better) , we should be concocting music as unpalatable as their libretti. . . .

your most obedient son

W. A. Mozart

12

David Boyden

1910-

LUDWIG VAN BEETHOVEN

[1956]

ANY DISCUSSION OF MUSIC in the nineteenth century must begin with Beethoven, for, like Monteverdi two centuries earlier, he bridges two eras. While the music of the eighteenth century played a formative role in Beethoven's early style, his last works are separated from those of Haydn and Mozart by a wide gulf— a gulf as pronounced as that which the rise of the middle class, the French Revolution, and Romanticism produced between the eighteenth and nineteenth centuries: Beethoven's greatness manifests itself in a force and intellect that required new styles and expanded forms to contain his ideas and emotions, and his example profoundly influenced all subsequent music.

Beethoven exhibited a new attitude toward society, and his position in contemporary Viennese society was quite different from that of Haydn and Mozart. A prouder and bolder spirit by nature than either of them, and imbued with the new ideas of the rights of man and the revolutionary idea of the pre-eminence of the artist, he treated the highest personages in society as equals from the beginning. Bettina Brentano, who numbered Goethe and Beethoven among her friends, suggested that Beethoven treated God as an equal. Although this gifted lady was a notoriously unreliable witness, the fact remains that Beethoven was on terms of friendship with the highest members of society, including Archduke Rudolf; and several of them, fearing that Beethoven might leave Vienna, settled on him an annuity of four thousand florins. Unlike Mozart, whose funeral was practically unattended and who was buried in a pauper's grave, Beethoven's funeral was attended by twenty thousand people from all ranks of Viennese society.

Like the music of many composers, that of Beethoven can be divided into three styles; in his case, however, this division has special significance because of his position between two centuries. The threefold division was made more than a hundred years ago (1852) by Wilhelm von Lenz, according to whom Beethoven's first style imitated Haydn and Mozart, the second showed his complete freedom from his models, and the third was a new, personal, and somewhat introspective style. These distinctions are useful if they are not taken too seriously. As a matter of fact, the distinctions are not strictly chronological, and Beethoven's works present special difficulties of classification because he worked with such care and concentration that each production is an individual and particular organism.

First period: to 1800, until Beethoven was thirty years old. Among the works in this period are the first six string quartets (Op. 18), the first eleven piano sonatas, and the first two symphonies.

Second period: 1800-15. This period includes the Third through the Eighth Symphonies, his only opera *Fidelio,* five string quartets (Op. 59, Op. 78, and Op. 95), the Violin Concerto, the Third, Fourth, and Fifth Piano Concertos, and Piano Sonatas No. 12 (Op. 26) to No. 27 (Op. 90).

Third period: 1815-27. This period embraces the greatest works of Beethoven: the last piano sonatas, the last five string quartets (starting with Op. 127), the Ninth Symphony, and the *Missa Solemnis.*

Did Beethoven really belong to the Romantic period? The Romantic period thought so, and almost every subsequent composer paid him tribute. Perhaps the situation is similar to that of Goethe, who thought of himself as a Classicist until Schiller attempted to prove that his *Iphigenie* put him with the Romanticists. Beethoven was imbued with the ideals of the time, the brotherhood of man, the heroic, and the rights of the individual. His very character was attuned to the stuff of the early nineteenth century, and his personal style of music was suited to the general expression of these sentiments. On the other hand, Beethoven was not basically inspired by the typical lyrical expression of Romanticism; he shared its literary penchant only in part; and his music does not really represent the "addition of strangeness to beauty." All these things can be found in Beethoven's music, but fundamentally they are peripheral to a hard core of musical logic applied, for the most part, to the instrumental forms of the Classic period expanded to their elastic limit and, in his last works, some times beyond.

Still, Beethoven's work contained the seeds of the Romantic spirit; and while he brought the Classic era to an end, he helped inspire Romanticism. Beethoven actually had far more influence on the Romantic composers than they on him; and those that followed tended to isolate phases of his work for their point of departure. In this sense Beethoven was a Romantic composer and the fountainhead of much of the instrumental music of Romanticism.

The symphonies are a case in point. Mendelssohn and Schumann were particularly influenced by the Fourth Symphony. The Sixth ("Pastoral") was most influential in the orchestral program music of Berlioz and Liszt, although Beethoven himself considered this symphony "more the expression of feeling than painting," and the programmatic elements, though prominent, are subordinate to the symphonic development. Schubert, and later Brahms, followed the general plan of the Third, Fifth, and Seventh Symphonies. The germs of a unified synthesis of an art work, the ideal of Liszt and Wagner, are found in Beethoven's Fifth and Ninth Symphonies. In the former the third and last movements are connected, and a substantial section from the third movement is quoted in the last. The final movement of the Ninth ("Choral") Symphony attempts another synthesis, that of soloists, chorus, and orchestra in an instrumental work. Beethoven begins this movement with quotations from the preceding movements, and then, having summarized and apparently rejected them, he proceeds to *incorporate* the vocal elements into the framework of the symphony itself. A number of other choral symphonies followed the advent of the Ninth Symphony, and Berlioz used the same procedure of summary and rejection in the last movement of his *Harold* Symphony, a purely instrumental work.

Beethoven was such a universal figure that he inspired whole generations, and not merely through the forms of the symphony. His fertility in development of material, so noticeable in his development sections in sonata form or in his variations, inspired Wagner; and the mature operas of the latter would not have been possible without Beethoven's technique of development. In a general way, his dramatic and dynamic style inspired those around him, and his imaginative and individual solutions bewildered as well as attracted a generation whose watchword was individuality. But his last and most profound works, the last five string quartets, have no direct descendants. It was not possible, for they are the most individual and personal expression of a great artist, withdrawn from life and tapping the deepest springs of his noblest thought and inexorable logic.[1]

Beethoven brought to music a greater emotional intensity

---

[1] Beethoven's withdrawal from life was undoubtedly occasioned by the total deafness of his last years. See Beethoven's own pathetic comments on his condition in the *Heiligenstadt Testament* of 1802. His deafness and family difficulties with his brothers and nephew were the great trials of his life.

than did either Haydn or Mozart. His heroic and dynamic style depends on the magnitude of his conceptions and on the driving power and elemental force with which they are executed. To achieve his ends, Beethoven expanded the previous range of louds and softs. The *sforzando* is used for various effects, some rhythmic, some harmonic, some dynamic, but always with the impression of a strong personal insistence on the point at issue. He took advantage of sharper dissonances for great harmonic contrast and for emotional intensity; and it is no mistake that some of these dissonances are emphasized by *sforzandi* to make the point even stronger. His modulations into more remote keys also give him the opportunity for greater contrast and for musical architecture on a grander scale. The listener is immediately impressed with the strength of the themes themselves and with the sheer power of the figuration of the accompanying parts. The rhythm, particularly, is always a driving force. It is one of the most interesting features of Beethoven's music; and in this respect Beethoven is one of the most imaginative composers. Rhythm is the single most dominating trait of certain works (the Seventh Symphony); and throughout his music the drive of the rhythm, the shifting of accent and meter, and the force of his syncopations are central to its titanic strength, its relentless movement, and it inexhaustible variety.

Compared with his models, Beethoven's music is more continuously and organically conceived. Compared with Mozart's music, his is less sectional; rather, each new section or theme is fused with what has already been heard. The process of development took on new significance with Beethoven, for the expansion of a musical idea was at the heart of his method and especially congenial to one of his imagination and flair for improvisation. Hence the development sections became central to the sonata form and the codas are frequently closing developments.

Beethoven's whole method of composition, as shown by his notebooks, was a relatively slow and painful one: a continuous search for melodic material of a hard gemlike core, which in turn could serve as germinal motives to develop a whole structure. This process was quite different from that of Mozart, who spoke of themes coming to him "from he knew not where," and "being able to see how to develop them." Such spontaneity of melodic inspiration is also characteristic of Schubert, but not of Beethoven.

Ernest Newman says of the Beethoven themes: "To assume that it was out of the themes that the movement grew is probably to see the process from the wrong end . . . the long and painful search for the themes was simply an effort, not to find workable atoms out of which he could construct a musical edifice according to the conventions of symphonic form, but to reduce an already existing nebula . . . to the atom, and then, by the orderly arrangement of these atoms, to make the implicit explicit. The themes are not the generator of the mass of music but are themselves rather the condensation of this.[2]

The inherited forms of the eighteenth century were gradually changed by Beethoven so that his later works are far removed from his models. He completely changed the old minuet, substituting the scherzo, so different in mood and rhythm. While Beethoven retained the outlines of the old concerto form of Mozart, there were important changes. The orchestra became a dominant force, and in his last concertos certain traditional features were abandoned. In his Fourth Piano Concerto (G major) the soloist, not the orchestra, opens the work; and in the Fifth ("Emperor") Concerto, the cadenza is written out—a practice that was generally followed thereafter.

The works of the last period in particular exhibit the most fanciful use of inherited forms, especially the fugue and the

[2] *The Unconscious Beethoven* (New York: Alfred A. Knopf, 1927).

variation. The "Great" Fugue (Op. 133), originally the last movement of the B-flat Quartet (Op. 130), is so extended and overpowering, that it was detached from the quartet and played as a separate piece. In his variations Beethoven displayed his enormous powers of fantasy and improvisation. A fondness for the variation was characteristic of him throughout his life (see the last movement of the *Eroica;* or the F major Variations which use different keys for the individual variations); however, in the variations of the last period—the "Diabelli" Variations for piano, those in the E-flat Quartet (Op. 127) and A minor Quartet (Op. 132), and in the last piano sonata—Beethoven proceeded beyond the previous limits established by Bach's "Goldberg" Variations and reached a point of achievement that is not likely to be surpassed.

Beethoven's continual search for new means of expression took many forms. He experimented with mixtures of forms (for instance, the sonata with the rondo), and he introduced voices into the Ninth Symphony and recitative-like passages into the piano sonata (Op. 31, No. 2; Op. 110) and string quartet (Op. 132, transition to the last movement). In the C-sharp Minor Quartet (Op. 131) Beethoven combined seven movements of which the first is a fugue, into a continuous whole.

Beethoven also increased the size of the orchestra. In the *Eroica* he added a third horn, and in the Ninth Symphony four horns are required. In the Fifth and Ninth Symphonies Beethoven achieves additional power and sonority with three trombones. The double bassoon is sometimes used, and in the Ninth Symphony, triangle, bass drum, and cymbals are added to the percussion. In his orchestration Beethoven gave the timpani increased prominence, assigning them thematic material in the Ninth Symphony. He emancipated the cello from the double bass, and treated it as a tenor as well as a bass. In this connection, one may cite the use of two solo celli in the second movement of the "Pastoral" Symphony.

Beethoven's importance in music cannot be overestimated. In his music, the listener feels the greatness of an elemental force, a composer of the very first magnitude. This is true in the sense that his music appeals directly to the listener because of its extraordinary power, intensity, and variety of emotional expression. It is also true in the historical sense. Some composers are born at the wrong time and place for the full realization of their potentialities (e.g., Purcell). Others, like Beethoven, come at precisely the right time. He lived when a new spirit of individuality and a spirit of revolt against the established order of things had permeated arts, letters, and politics Temperamentally, he was in tune with the spirit of his era, and he possessed the supreme ability to articulate the deepest thoughts and aspirations of people everywhere. Beethoven brought to logical fruition the models he had inherited from Haydn and Mozart. But he also reflected a new spirit, especially in his late works, and his music is the portal through which one must approach the nineteenth century and the Romantic movement in music. For similar reasons, Beethoven had an immense influence on the future course of music in the nineteenth century. Above all, whatever Beethoven's historical importance may have been, he has never become old-fashioned; and that in itself is the supreme tribute to the universality of genius.

13

Ludwig van Beethoven

1770-1827

TWO LETTERS TO HIS PUBLISHER,
BREITKOPF AND HÄRTEL

VIENNA, *July* 13, 1802

— — — As to the works to be arranged I am heartily delighted that you have refused them. The *unnatural mania,* now so prevalent, for transferring even *pianoforte compositions* to stringed instruments, instruments which in all respects are so utterly different from one another, should really be checked. I firmly maintain that only *Mozart* could arrange for other instruments the works he composed for the pianoforte; and *Haydn* could do this too—And without wishing to force my company on those two great men. I make the same statement about *my own pianoforte sonatas also,* for not only would whole passages have to be entirely omitted or altered, but some would have to—be added; and there one finds the nasty stumbling-block, to *overcome which one must either be the composer himself* or at any rate possess the same *skill and inventiveness* —I have arranged only one of my sonatas for string quartet,[1] because I was so earnestly implored to do so; and I am quite convinced that nobody else could do the same thing with ease.

[1] His piano sonata in E major, Op. 14, No. 1.—*Ed.*

[VIENNA, *October* 18,1802]

As my brother is writing to you, I am just adding the following information—I have composed two sets of variations, one consisting of eight variations and the other of thirty. Both sets are worked out in quite a *new manner,* and each in a *separate and different way.* I would infinitely prefer to have them engraved by you, *but on no other condition than for a fee of 50 ducats for both sets*[2]—Do not let me make this offer in vain, for I assure you that you will have no regrets in respect of these two works—*Each theme is treated in its own way and in a different way from the other one.* Usually I have to wait for other people to tell me when I have new ideas, because I never know this myself. But this time—I myself can assure you that in both these works the *method is quite new so far as I am concerned*—

What you wrote to me once about the *endeavour to sell my works I cannot endorse.* Surely it is an outstanding proof of *the excellent sale of my works* that nearly all *foreign publishers* are continually writing to me for compositions, and that even *those who pirate engraved works,* about whom you rightly complain, *are to be found among this number.* Why, Simrock has already written to me a few times for compositions which he alone would like to possess; and he is willing to pay me whatever any other publisher offers—You may regard it as a kind of favour that I myself have made you this offer *before making it to anyone else,* the reason being that *your behaviour* has always merited this distinction—

Your

L. VAN BEETHOVEN

[2] Opp. 34 and 35.—*Ed.*

14

Ludwig van Beethoven

1770-1827

~~~

HEILIGENSTADT TESTAMENT

FOR MY BROTHERS CARL AND—BEETHOVEN

O ye men who regard or declare me to be malignant, stubborn or cynical, how unjust are ye towards me. You do not know the secret cause of my seeming so. From childhood onward, my heart and mind prompted me to be kind and tender, and I was ever inclined to accomplish great deeds. But only think that during the last six years, I have been in a wretched condition, rendered worse by unintelligent physicians. Deceived from year to year with hopes of improvement, and then finally forced to the prospect of *lasting infirmity* (which may last for years, or even be totally incurable). Born with a fiery, active temperament, even susceptive of the diversions of society, I had soon to retire from the world, to live a solitary life. At times, even, I endeavoured to forget all this, but how harshly was I driven back by the redoubled experience of my bad hearing. Yet it was not possible for me to say to men: Speak louder, shout, for I am deaf. Alas! how could I declare the weakness of a *sense* which in me *ought to be* more acute than in others—a sense which *formerly* I possessed in highest perfection, a perfection such as few in my profession enjoy, or ever have enjoyed; no I cannot do it. Forgive, therefore, if you see me withdraw, when I would willingly mix with you. My misfortune pains me doubly, in that I am certain to be misunderstood. For me there can be no recreation in the society of my fellow creatures, no refined conversations, no interchange of thought. Almost alone, and only mixing in society when absolutely necessary, I am compelled to live as an exile. If I approach near to people, a feeling of hot anxiety comes over me lest my condition should be noticed—for so it was during these past six months which I spent in the country. Ordered by my intelligent physician to spare my hearing as much as possible, he almost fell in with my present frame of mind, although many a time I was carried away by my sociable inclinations. But how humiliating was it, when some one standing close to me heard a distant flute, and I heard *nothing,* or a *shepherd singing,* and again I heard nothing. Such incidents almost drove me to despair; at times I was on the point of putting an end to my life—*art* alone restrained my hand. Oh! it seemed as if I could not quit this earth until I had produced all I felt within me, and so I continued this wretched life— wretched, indeed, with so sensitive a body that a somewhat sudden change can throw me from the best into the worst state. *Patience,* I am told, I must choose as my guide. I have done so—lasting, I hope, will be my resolution to bear up until it pleases the inexorable Parcae to break the thread. Forced already in my 28th year to become a philosopher, it is not easy; for an artist more difficult than for any one else. O Divine Being, Thou who lookest down into my inmost soul, Thou understandest; Thou knowest that love for mankind and a desire to do good dwell therein. Oh, my fellow men, when one day you read this, remember that you were unjust to me, and let the unfortunate one console himself if he can find one like himself, who in spite of all obstacles which nature has thrown in his way, has still done everything in his power to be received into the ranks of worthy artists and men. You, my

95

brothers Carl and—, as soon as I am dead, beg Professor Schmidt, if he be still living, to describe my malady; and annex this written account to that of my illness, so that at least the world, so far as is possible, may become reconciled to me after my death. And now I declare you both heirs to my small fortune (if such it may be called). Divide it honourably and dwell in peace, and help each other. What you have done against me, has, as you know, long been forgiven. And you, brother Carl, I especially thank you for the attachment you have shown towards me of late. My prayer is that your life may be better, less troubled by cares, than mine. Recommend to your children *virtue;* it alone can bring happiness, not money. I speak from experience. It was virtue which bore me up in time of trouble; to her, next to my art, I owe thanks for my not having laid violent hands on myself. Farewell, and love one another. My thanks to all friends, especially *Prince Lichnowski and Professor Schmidt.* I should much like one of you to keep as an heirloom the instruments given to me by Prince L., but let no strife arise between you concerning them; if money should be of more service to you, just sell them. How happy I feel that even when lying in my grave, I may be useful to you.

So let it be. I joyfully hasten to meet death. If it come before I have had opportunity to develop all my artistic faculties, it will come, my hard fate notwithstanding, too soon, and I should probably wish it later—yet even then I shall be happy, for will it not deliver me from a state of endless suffering? Come when thou wilt, I shall face thee courageously—farewell, and when I am dead do not entirely forget me. This I deserve from you, for during my lifetime I often thought of you, and how to make you happy. Be ye so.

LUDWIG VAN BEETHOVEN

Heiglnstadt, the 6th of October, 1802

[*Black seal*]

[On the fourth side of the great Will sheet]

Heiglnstadt, October, 1802, thus I take my farewell of thee
—and indeed sadly—yes, that fond hope which I entertained
when I came here, of being at any rate healed up to a certain
point, must be entirely abandoned. As the leaves of autumn
fall and fade, so it has withered away for me; almost the same
as when I came here do I go away—even the High courage
which often in the beautiful summer days quickened me, that
has vanished. O Providence, let me have just one pure day of
joy; so long is it since true joy filled my heart. Oh when, oh
when, oh Divine Being, shall I be able once again to feel it in
the temple of nature and of men. Never—no—that would be
too hard.

For my brothers Carl and — to execute after my death.

THE ROMANTIC ERA

15

Donald Jay Grout

1902-

THE NATURE OF ROMANTICISM

IN MUSIC HISTORY, the Romantic period is regarded as equivalent
to the nineteenth century, with the understanding that certain
Romantic traits are evident in the music of the latter part of
the eighteenth century and others persist in various guises into
the twentieth century. In accepting this concept, our first task
must be to define as clearly as possible what we mean by
Romantic with reference to music of the nineteenth century;
having done this, we shall examine the principal types of vocal,
instrumental, and operatic compositions of the period. In the
course of our survey it will become clear that the Romantic
movement includes a great variety of styles and that within its
general unity there are many contradictions and counter currents.

The adjective *romantic* comes from *romance,* which had an
original literary meaning of a medieval tale or poem treating
heroic personages or events and written in one of the Romance
languages—that is, one of the vernacular languages descended
from Latin ("Roman"). The medieval poems dealing with King
Arthur were called the Arthurian romances, for example.
Hence, when the word *romantic* first came into use around the
middle of the seventeenth century it carried the connotation of
something far off, legendary, fictitious, fantastic, and marvelous, an imaginary or ideal world which was contrasted with the

actual world of the present. This connotation is the basis of Walter Pater's definition of Romanticism as "the addition of strangeness to beauty," and is hinted in Lord Bacon's dictum that "there is no excellent beauty that hath not some strangeness in the proportion."

In a very general sense, all art may be said to be Romantic; for, though it may take its materials from actual life, it transforms them and thus creates a new world which is necessarily to a greater or lesser degree remote from the everyday world. From this point of view, Romantic art differs from Classic art by its greater emphasis on the qualities of remoteness and strangeness, with all that such emphasis may imply as to choice and treatment of material. Romanticism, in this general sense, is not a phenomenon of any one period, but has occurred at various times in various forms. It is possible to see in the history of music, and of the other arts, alternating periods of Classicism and Romanticism—or, as Curt Sachs calls them, cycles of *ethos* and *pathos;* thus the *ars nova* may be considered Romantic in comparison with the *ars antiqua,* or the Baroque in comparison with the Renaissance, in somewhat the same way that the nineteenth century is Romantic in comparison with the Classicism of the eighteenth century.

Another fundamental trait of Romanticism is boundlessness, in two different though related senses. First, Romantic art aspires to transcend immediate times or occasions, to seize eternity, to reach back into the past and forward into the future, to range over the expanse of the world and outward through the cosmos. As against the classic ideals of order, equilibrium, control, and perfection within acknowledged limits, Romanticism cherishes freedom, movement, passion, and endless pursuit of the unattainable. And just because its goal can never be attained, Romantic art is haunted by a spirit of longing, of yearning after an impossible fulfillment.

Second, the Romantic impatience of limits leads to a breaking down of distinctions. The personality of the artist tends to become merged with the work of art; Classical clarity is replaced by a certain intentional obscurity, definite statement by suggestion, allusion, or symbol. The arts themselves tend to merge; poetry, for example, aims to acquire the qualities of music, and music the characteristics of poetry.

If remoteness and boundlessness are Romantic, then music is the most Romantic of the arts. Its material—ordered sound and rhythm—is almost completely detached from the concrete world of objects, and this very detachment makes music most apt at suggesting the flood of impressions, thoughts, and feelings which is the proper domain of Romantic art. Obviously only instrumental music—pure music free from the burden of words—can perfectly attain this goal of communicating emotion. Instrumental music, therefore, is the ideal Romantic art. Its detachment from the world, its mystery, and its incomparable power of suggestion which works on the mind directly without the mediation of words, made it the dominant art of the Romantic period. "All art constantly aspires towards the condition of music," wrote Pater. Schopenhauer believed that music was the very image and incarnation of the innermost reality of the world, the immediate expression of the universal feelings and impulsions of life in concrete, definite form.

At this point we come upon the first of several apparently opposing conditions that beset all attempts to grasp the meaning of *Romantic* as applied to the music of the nineteenth century. We shall endeavor to deal with this difficulty by summarizing the conflicting tendencies that affected the music of the time and noting in what way the musicians of the Romantic period sought to harmonize these oppositions in their own thought and practice.

The first opposition involves the relation between music and words. If instrumental music is the perfect Romantic art, why is it that the acknowledged great masters of the symphony, the highest form of instrumental music, were not Romantics, but were the Classical composers, Haydn, Mozart, and Beethoven? Moreover, one of the most characteristic Romantic forms was the Lied, a vocal piece, in which Schubert, Schumann Brahms, and Hugo Wolf attained a new and intimate union between music and poetry. Even the instrumental music of most Romantic composers was dominated by the lyrical spirit of the Lied rather than the dramatic-epic spirit of the symphony, as exemplified in the later works of Mozart and Haydn and above all in Beethoven. Furthermore, a large number of the leading Romantic composers were extraordinarily articulate and interested in literary expression, and many leading Romantic novelists and poets wrote about music with deep love and insight. The novelist E. T. A. Hoffmann was a successful composer of operas; Weber, Schumann, and Berlioz wrote distinguished essays on music; Wagner was a poet, essayist, and philosopher as well as a composer.

The conflict between the ideal of pure instrumental music as the supremely Romantic mode of expression on the one hand, and the strong literary orientation of Romantic music on the other, was resolved in the conception of *program music*. Program music, as the nineteenth century used the term, was instrumental music associated with poetic, descriptive, or even narrative subject matter—not by means of conventional musical figures (as in the Baroque era) or by imitation of natural sounds and movements (as in the eighteenth century), but by means of imaginative suggestion. Program music aimed to absorb and transmute the imagined subject, taking it wholly into the dimension of music in such a way that the resulting composition, while it includes the "program," nevertheless completely dominates it and is in a certain sense independent of it. Instrumental music thus becomes a vehicle for the utterance of thoughts which, though they may be hinted in words, are ultimately beyond the power of words to express. A second way in which the Romantics reconciled music with words is reflected in the importance they placed on the instrumental accompaniment of vocal music, from the *Lieder* of Schubert to the symphonic orchestra that enfolds the voices in Wagner's music dramas.

The starting point for Romantic program music was Beethoven's *Pastoral* Symphony. The composers most explicitly committed to program music in the early and middle nineteenth century were Mendelssohn, Schumann, Berlioz, and Liszt, while its chief representatives at the end of the century were Debussy and Richard Strauss. But practically every composer of the Romantic era was, to a greater or lesser degree, writing program music, whether or not he publicly acknowledged it; and one reason why it is so easy for listeners to connect a scene or a story or a poem with a piece of Romantic music is that often the composer himself, perhaps unconsciously, was working from some such idea. Romantic writers on music projected their own conceptions of the expressive function of music into the past, and read Romantic programs into the instrumental works not only of Beethoven but also of Mozart, Haydn, and Bach .

Another area of conflict involved the relationship between the composer and his audience. The transition from relatively small, homogeneous, and cultured audiences for music to the huge, diverse, and relatively unprepared middle-class public of the Romantic period had already begun in the eighteenth century. The disappearance of individual patronage and the rapid growth of concert societies and musical festivals in the early part of the nineteenth century were signs of this change. The Romantic composers, if they were to succeed, somehow had to reach the vast new audience; their struggle to be heard and understood had to occur in an incomparably larger arena than at any previous epoch in the history of music. Yet it is the Romantic period more than any other that offers us the phenomenon of the unsociable artist, one who feels himself to be separate from his fellow-men and who is driven by isolation to seek inspiration within himself. These Romantic musicians did not compose, as did their eighteenth-century forebears, for a patron or for a particular function, but for infinity, for posterity, for some imaginable ideal audience which, they hoped, would some day understand and appreciate them; either that, or they wrote for a little circle of kindred spirits, confessing to them those inmost feelings considered too fragile and precious to be set before the crude public of the concert halls. This is the basis for the contrast, so typical of the Romantic era, between the grandiose creations of Meyerbeer, Berlioz, Wagner, Strauss, or Mahler on the one hand and the intimate lyrical effusions of Schumann's *Lieder* or Schubert's, Mendelssohn's, and Chopin's short piano pieces on the other.

The gulf between the mass audience and the lonely composer could not always be bridged. Facile musicians with a knack for pleasing the public turned out reams of trivial or bombastic salon music, but conscientious artists despised such vulgarity. Partly in sheer self-defense, as compensation, they were driven to the conception of the composer as an exalted combination of priest and poet, one to whom it was given to reveal to mankind the deeper meaning of life through the divine medium of music. The artist was a "genius" who wrote under "inspiration," a prophet even though his message might be rejected.

In the third part of Novalis' novel *Heinrich von Ofterdingen* (1802) there is a story that illustrates the Romantic ideal of the artist: a humble young woodsman secretly weds a princess, and a child is born to them. They come with trepidation to seek reconciliation with the king, the princess' father. The king receives them and their child with joy, amid the approving shouts of the populace. Undoubtedly the climax of this tale represents allegorically the public acceptance and triumph which the Romantic artist always longed for but did not always obtain. If his will and energy were sufficient he might come to dominate the popular imagination, as Beethoven had done, as Berlioz struggled to do, and as Liszt and Wagner did on an unprecedented scale. It is remarkable that the great virtuoso performers of the nineteenth century were dominating, heroic individuals—for example, Paganini and Liszt. They were instrumental soloists, as opposed to the typical eighteenth-century virtuoso, the operatic singer, who was the most conspicuous member of a group, and the typical twentieth-century virtuoso, the conductor, who is the dictator of a group. This accent on the individual is present everywhere in Romanticism: the best vocal music of the period is for solo voice, not for chorus. This conception of the composer as a prophet, a heroic figure struggling against a hostile environment, also served to lend the music a quality of excitement, an emotional tension by means of which the audience was stimulated and uplifted.

Partly because of the industrial revolution, the population of Europe increased tremendously during the nineteenth century. Most of the increase occurred in cities: the populations of both London and Paris quadrupled between 1800 and 1880. Consequently, the majority of people, including the majority of musicians, no longer lived in a community, a court or town, where everybody knew everybody else and the open countryside was never very far away; instead, they were lost in the huge impersonal huddle of a modern city.

But the more man's daily life became separated from Nature, the more he became enamoured of Nature. From Rousseau onward, nature was idealized, and increasingly so in its wilder and more picturesque aspects. The nineteenth century was an age of landscape painting. . . . A kinship was felt between the inner life of the artist and the life of Nature, so that the latter became not only a refuge but also a source of strength, inspiration, and revelation. This mystic sense of kinship with Nature, counterbalancing the artificiality of city existence, is as prevalent in the music of the nineteenth century as it is in the contemporary literature and art.

The nineteenth century saw a rapid expansion in exact knowledge and scientific method. Simultaneously, as though in reaction, the music of the Romantic era is constantly thrusting beyond the borders of the rational into the unconscious and the supernatural. It takes its subject material from the dream (the individual unconscious), as in Berlioz's *Symphonie fantastique,* or from the myth (the collective unconscious), as in Wagner's music dramas. Even Nature itself is haunted in the Romantic imagination by spirits and is fraught with mysterious significances. The effort to find a musical language capable of expressing these new and strange ideas led to new worlds of harmony, melody, and orchestral color . . .

Another area of conflict in the nineteenth century was political: it was the conflict between the growth of nationalism and the beginning of supranational socialist movements outlined by the *Communist Manifesto* of Marx and Engels (1848), and Marx's *Capital* (1867). Nationalism was an important influence in Romantic music. Differences between national musical styles were accentuated and folk song came to be venerated as the spontaneous expression of the national soul. Musical Romanticism flourished especially in Germany, not only because the Romantic temper was congenial to German ways of thinking, but also because in that country national sentiment, being for a long time suppressed politically, had to find vent in music and other forms of art. Supplementary to the concentration on national music was a delight in exoticism, the sympathetic use of foreign idioms for picturesque color. The music of the great Romantic composers was not, of course, limited to any one country; what it had to say was addressed to all humanity. But its idioms were national when compared with the eighteenth-century ideal of a cosmopolitan musical language in which national peculiarities were minimized.

The Romantic movement had from the beginning a revolutionary tinge, with a corresponding emphasis on the virtue of originality in art. Romanticism was seen as a revolt against the limitations of Classicism, although at the same time music was regarded as exemplifying the prevalent conception that the nineteenth century was an era of progress and evolution.

Composers up to the end of the eighteenth century had written for their own time, for the present; by and large they were neither much interested in the past nor much concerned about the future. But the Romantic composers, feeling the present unsympathetic, took an appeal to the judgment of posterity; it is not altogether coincidence that two of Wagner's essays on music were entitled *Art and Revolution* (1849) and *The Art-Work of the Future* (1850). With respect to the immediate past, however, the revolutionary aspect was overshadowed by the conception of Romanticism as the fulfillment of Classicism. The *empfindsamer Stil* and *Sturm und Drang* tendencies of the 1770's, which from our vantage point we can see as early manifestations of the Romantic movement, were not much regarded; but Beethoven and, to some extent, Mozart also were viewed by the Romantic composers as having marked out the path which they themselves were to follow. Thus arose the concept of music as an art that had a history—moreover, a history which was to be interpreted, in accord with the dominant philosophical ideas of the time, as a process of evolution.

The past was manifested in Romantic music by the persistence of the Classical tradition. Composers still wrote in the Classical forms of sonata, symphony, and string quartet; the Classical system of harmony was still the basis of Romantic music. Moreover, not all the Romantic composers went the whole way in adopting Romantic innovations; there were conservatives and radicals within the general movement. Mendelssohn, Brahms, and Bruckner were conservative; Berlioz, Liszt, and Wagner were more radical. Conservative and radical tendencies existed side by side in Schumann.

One of the most striking aspects of the Romantic movement

is its affinity with Bach and Palestrina, its conscious preoccupation with the remote past, something previously unknown in the history of music. Bach's *Passion According to St. Matthew* was revived in a performance at Berlin under Mendelssohn's direction in 1829; this performance was one conspicuous example of a general interest in Bach's music, which led in 1850 to the beginning of the publication of the first complete edition of his works. A similar edition of Palestrina's works was begun in 1862. The rapid rise of historical musicology in the nineteenth century was another outgrowth of the Romantic interest in the music of former ages, while the discoveries of musicologists further stimulated such interest. The Romantics, of course, romanticized history; they heard in the music of Bach, Palestrina, and other older composers what it suited them to hear, and adopted such things as they wanted for their own purposes. It was not the least of the many contradictions within the Romantic movement that its subjectively motivated reach into the past should have opened the way to the objective discipline of historical research in music.

The meaning of *Romantic* as applied to the music of the nineteenth century is not to be found in any single statement. Romanticism was a style, or rather a complex of many individual styles having elements in common, developed by musicians who had to resolve certain basic conflicts betwen their art and their environment. Similar conflicts may have existed in earlier periods, but in the Romantic period, for the first time, composers were forced publicly and continuously to come to grips with them. The nature of the issues, the urgency of the challenge, and the character of the response were peculiar to the nineteenth century. The Romantic style in music was the result. . . .

A few general observations may be made about the technical differences between Romantic and Classical music. On the whole, Romantic rhythms are less vital and less varied than those of the earlier period; interest is directed rather to lyrical melody. Highly developed Classical forms, like the symphony or sonata, are handled less satisfactorily by the Romantics. A piano sonata by Chopin or Schumann, for example, is like a novel by Tieck or Novalis—a series of picturesque episodes without any strong bond of unity within the work. Quite often, however, a Romantic symphony or oratorio aimed at achieving a new kind of unity by means of thematic transformation or by using the same themes in different movements. The Romantic treatment of shorter forms is usually quite simple and clear.

The most remarkable Romantic achievements lay in the development of harmonic technique and instrumental color. There was a continuous increase of harmonic complexity throughout the nineteenth century. Chromatic harmonies, chromatic voice leading, distant modulations, complex chords, freer use of nonharmonic tones, and a growing tendency to avoid distinct cadences on the tonic, all operated to extend and blur the outlines of tonality. Romantic harmony as a means of expression went hand in hand with an ever-expanding palette of color. New sonorities were discovered in piano music; new instruments were added to the orchestra, and older instruments were redesigned to be more sonorous and more flexible; above all, new combinations of instruments in the ensemble were invented to produce new color effects. A sign of the times was the appearance in 1844 of Berlioz's *Treatise on Instrumentation and Orchestration,* the first textbook of any importance on this subject that had ever been published. Harmony and color were the principal means whereby the nineteenth-century composers sought to express in music the Romantic ideals of remoteness, ardor, and boundless longing.

16

Alfred Einstein

1880-1952

MUSIC AS THE CENTER OF THE ARTS

(Selections from *Music in the Romantic Era*)

Critic and musicologist (and cousin of Albert), Alfred Einstein's writings include original contributions in all areas of music history, e.g. *The Italian Madrigal* (1949), *Mozart, His Character, His Work* (1945), and *Music in the Romantic Era* (1947).

THE 18TH CENTURY had tried to *separate* the arts. True, Lessing, one of the most clearheaded men of his time, was not favorably disposed towards Rationalism. He was an opponent of the neatly-measured-off "Classical" French tragedy with its three unities and exhibited a particular dislike for Voltaire, while admiring the "rule-less" Shakespeare. His love of the unconventional permitted fresh air to stream into the dusty chambers of German literature. Yet he advocated in his most significant essay on art, the *Laocoön*, a strict separation of the pictorial and the poetic, and drew for both areas as sharply as possible the boundary-lines of what was there representable. Had he lived longer (he died in 1781), he would have resisted passionately the intrusion of the "musical" into poetry and painting, on the grounds that it was a mysterious, disruptive, uncontrollable ingredient. Here also he would have insisted upon clear separation and would have sharply put music in its place.

112

To the Romantics, however, the arts merged into one. This tendency was so strong that it could not be resisted even by certain very great spirits born and reared in the clear air of the 18th century. Both Schiller and Goethe looked with some envy on the nature and development of opera; Mozart's *Don Giovanni* made a deep impression on Schiller, *The Magic Flute,* a deep impression on Goethe—so deep that he tried his hand at a continuation, a second part. It is significant that this period straightway supplied musical background for Shakespeare's later works, particularly *The Tempest,* which has much in common with *The Magic Flute.* More than once *The Tempest* was reworked into an opera. What is the second part of Goethe's *Faust* but the literary counterpart to a "magic opera"—to, one might almost say, a "grand opera"? At all events, it is impossible to think of *Faust II,* or to present it, without music.

Music and Word

If the great "Classics" of German literature were unable to avoid the Romantic trend towards music, the genuine Romantics actually regarded music as the primal cause, the very womb from which all the arts sprang and to which they were again to return. There was no poet of the Romantic era who did not think of his artistic medium—language—as inadequate. "O lovers," cried Ludwig Tieck, one of the founding fathers of Romanticism, "never forget, when you would entrust a sentiment to words, to ask yourselves: what, after all, is there that can be said in words!" Music, the mysterious force, stirring every depth, bursting every form, seemed alone capable of making the ultimate, the most direct statement. There was virtually a general flight of the Romantics into the ostensibly indefinite, engulfing depths of music.

Not only in Germany but also in England and France, the Romantic poets strove to create a new verbal music—at best, to strengthen the musical pulsation with which every genuine lyric is animated; at worst, to be satisfied with the sheer sound of the words, the play of vowels and consonants. The more "musical" a poem, the surer seemed to be its advance into new, unexplored regions of feeling. Limits melted away, not only between poetry and music, but also between music and painting. We must not be surprised, then, if E. T. A. Hoffmann gives definitive expression to the point of view in his famous critique of Beethoven's C-minor Symphony: "Music is the most Romantic of all the arts—in fact, it might almost be said to be the sole *purely* Romantic one."

The contrast with the 18th century in this respect could not have been more sharply drawn, the metamorphosis that took place in the very meaning of music more distinctly marked. Music became a medium through which the ineffable could be made palpable to sense, through which the mysterious, magical, and exciting could be created. To the great philosopher of the 18th century, Immanuel Kant, "nature" had been something hostile, the overcoming of which was one of the tasks of ethics. Along with his English predecessors and most of his contemporaries, he harbored a rationalistic mistrust of the unconscious, the subconscious, the impulsive. Even music had to be clear, formal, orderly, restrained. But the Romantics began to respect the unconscious; they began to relax the form; they let the reins hang loose. And they honored Beethoven because he seemed to them to have shattered clear form—one of their great misconceptions and misinterpretations—and because he seemed to have opened up for them not only unknown but also uncontrollable regions of feeling and agitation.

They honored Beethoven for still another reason: that he was so great and substantial an *instrumental* composer—and, as a matter of fact, the instrumental portion of Beethoven's creative activity does by far exceed the vocal. Just as the Romantics considered music the center, the kernel, the fountainhead of all the arts, so also did they think of purely instrumental composition as the center of all music. They did so, moreover, precisely because of the seemingly indefinite, ambiguous nature of music for instruments. They felt at the same time the necessity of investing music with a new comprehensibility, through a new convergence and amalgamation with poetry: through program music.

Yet, be it noted, this fusion was to take place along a new way. In all periods of history, of course, there has been program music. But Romantic program music has little in common with the program music of earlier times. The older program music was quite childlike in its attempt at pictorial representation; frequently it consisted only of a mere fanciful title. It was happy to take its cues from the most immediate associations of the audible: tumult of battle, bird-song, peal of bells, or thunderstorm and pastoral sounds. These composers still continued to preserve the limits of form, keeping within the framework of the sonata, the concerto grosso, or the symphony; and—what is more important—they addressed themselves to the clear, serene intellect of the listener. To use an 18th-century expression, there was more "play of wit and understanding."

Here again Beethoven put a new face on things. With his *Pastoral* Symphony and his sonata *Les Adieux,* he addressed himself more to the listener's feelings. This became the pattern for Romantic program music, except for the addition of a new ingredient, stimulus from literature.

The Romantic composer was no longer, so to speak, his own poet, but sought incitement to composition in the sister art of poetry: for example, Berlioz in Victor Hugo's Romantic thrillers, in Lord Byron's *Weltschmerz*-tinted scenes, in Sir Walter Scott's novels, and in Shakespeare's dramas. Liszt, moreover, summoned to his aid not only literature—Victor Hugo, Lamartine, Schiller, Goethe, Dante, Tasso, Shakespeare—but also painting. Liszt was even of the opinion that in the symphonic poem a more intimate union of poetry and music might be possible than in song, oratorio, or opera.

From time immemorial the sung word has occasioned or developed a *connection* between music and literary or quasi-literary works. The present attempt, however, is intended as a *fusion* of the two, which promises to become more intimate than any heretofore achieved. More and more the masterpieces of music will absorb the masterpieces of literature. After all that has been said and after music has developed so far in the modern era, we ask ourselves, "Is it possible that this fusion—which unmistakably has blossomed out from a modern way of feeling and from the connection of music with poetry—could become harmful? On what grounds should music, which was so inseparably associated with Sophocles's tragedies and Pindar's odes, hesitate at the thought of becoming fused—differently, but yet more fittingly—with literary works of post-Classical inspiration, of becoming identified with names such as Dante and Shakespeare?"

Whatever the validity of these pontifical assertions and rhetorical questions, they are characteristic of a tendency on the part of the Romantics to wipe out the boundary-lines between music and poetry. Music assumed a position, however, in these programmatic symphonies and "symphonic poems" (what a characteristic title!) not, as it were, in the service of poetry. Quite the contrary: music, it was felt, was doing a favor to poetry in trying to represent by more direct, sensuous, striking means what was ostensibly the essence of the poem or painting. What happened was a complicated matter, at once egoistic and altruistic. But if it was an egoistic act, designed to further music's best interests, yet it was one committed in good faith. It involved, at all events, a mixture of literary and musical elements, unthinkable for the 18th century and typically Romantic. In the new program music the Romantics again showed clearly that, for them, the limits of the arts were dissolved, but that within the combinations resulting from this strange alchemy, music was always the stronger element—the expressive center.

A similar mixing and shifting of the musical components in a quasi-chemical change took place in Romantic opera. True, the rule of music over drama had been established for almost two hundred years in Italian opera, and while occasionally it was made the subject of apparent controversy, for example by Gluck, in actuality, this hegemony had not for an instant faltered. Drama, the libretto of Italian opera, made no attempt whatsoever to shatter the bonds of its serfdom; it knew that the success of the opera depended entirely on the quality and achievement of the composer and the singers. In this relationship Romantic opera also made no change, although it felt that it was in fundamental opposition to its Italian rival. This was so because Romantic opera also discerned and acknowledged the overwhelming might, the superior power of music in the complicated whole of opera. Nothing was really changed in this situation by Wagner's demand that in opera the drama must have supremacy over the music, and that music should be the feminine, drama the masculine principle. The effect of his own work gives the lie to his theory, for this effect rests almost entirely on the music. The only difference is that, in the Wagnerian music drama, it was no longer the singer who bore the brunt of the expression, but the symphonically enlivened orchestra.

17

Ernst Theodor Amadeus Hoffmann

1776-1822

BEETHOVEN'S INSTRUMENTAL MUSIC

Best remembered for his tales of the grotesque and the supernatural, Hoffmann was also a composer, opera director, and
one of the founders of modern musical journalism. His work
had a profound influence on later Romanticists, both literary
and musical. The present selection appeared originally as two
reviews in 1810 and 1813.

WHEN WE SPEAK of music as an independent art, should we not
always restrict our meaning to instrumental music, which,
scorning every aid, every admixture of another art (the art of
poetry), gives pure expression to music's specific nature, recognizable in this form alone? It is the most romantic of all the
arts—one might almost say, the only genuinely romantic one
—for its sole subject is the infinite. The lyre of Orpheus opened
the portals of Orcus—music disclosed to man an unknown
realm, a world that has nothing in common with the external
sensual world that surrounds him, a world in which he leaves
behind him all definite feelings to surrender himself to an
inexpressible longing.

Have you even so much as suspected this specific nature, you
miserable composers of instrumental music, you who have
laboriously strained yourselves to represent definite emotions,
even definite events? How can it ever have occurred to you to
treat after the fashion of the plastic arts the art diametrically

opposed to plastic? Your sunrises, your tempests, your *Batailles des trois Empereurs*,[1] and the rest, these, after all, were surely quite laughable aberrations, and they have been punished as they well deserved by being wholly forgotten.

In song, where poetry, by means of words, suggests definite emotions, the magic power of music acts as does the wondrous elixir of the wise, a few drops of which make any drink more palatable and more lordly. Every passion—love, hatred, anger, despair, and so forth, just as the opera gives them to us —is clothed by music with the purple luster of romanticism, and even what we have undergone in life guides us out of life into the realm of the infinite.

As strong as this is music's magic, and, growing stronger and stronger, it had to break each chain that bound it to another art.

That gifted composers have raised instrumental music to its present high estate is due, we may be sure, less to the more readily handled means of expression (the greater perfection of the instruments, the greater virtuosity of the players) than to the more profound, more intimate recognition of music's specific nature.

Mozart and Haydn, the creators of our present instrumental music, were the first to show us the art in its full glory; the man who then looked on it with all his love and penetrated its innermost being is—Beethoven! The instrumental compositions of these three masters breathe a similar romantic spirit—this is due to their similar intimate understanding of the specific nature of the art; in the character of their compositions there is none the less a marked difference.

In Haydn's writing there prevails the expression of a serene and childlike personality. His symphonies lead us into vast green

---

[1] Perhaps Hoffmann is thinking of Louis Jadin's "La grande bataille d'Austerlitz," published in an arrangement for the piano by Kühnel of Leipzig in 1807 or earlier.—*Transl.*

woodlands, into a merry, gaily colored throng of happy mortals. Youths and maidens float past in a circling dance; laughing children, peering out from behind the trees, from behind the rose bushes, pelt one another playfully with flowers. A life of love, of bliss like that before the Fall, of eternal youth; no sorrow, no suffering, only a sweet melancholy yearning for the beloved object that floats along, far away, in the glow of the sunset and comes no nearer and does not disappear—nor does night fall while it is there, for it is itself the sunset in which hill and valley are aglow.

Mozart leads us into the heart of the spirit realm. Fear takes us in its grasp, but without torturing us, so that it is more an intimation of the infinite. Love and melancholy call to us with lovely spirit voices; night comes on with a bright purple luster, and with inexpressible longing we follow those figures which, waving us familiarly into their train, soar through the clouds in eternal dances of the spheres.[2]

Thus Beethoven's instrumental music opens up to us also the realm of the monstrous and the immeasurable. Burning flashes of light shoot through the deep night of this realm, and we become aware of giant shadows that surge back and forth, driving us into narrower and narrower confines until they destroy *us*—but not the pain of that endless longing in which each joy that has climbed aloft in jubilant song sinks back and is swallowed up, and it is only in this pain, which consumes love, hope, and happiness but does not destroy them, which seeks to burst our breasts with a many-voiced consonance of all the passions, that we live on, enchanted beholders of the supernatural!

Romantic taste is rare, romantic talent still rarer, and this is doubtless why there are so few to strike that lyre whose sound discloses the wondrous realm of the romantic.

---

[2] Mozart's Symphony in E-flat major, known as the "Swan Song."

Haydn grasps romantically what is human in human life; he is more commensurable, more comprehensible for the majority.

Mozart calls rather for the superhuman, the wondrous element that abides in inner being.

Beethoven's music sets in motion the lever of fear, of awe, of horror, of suffering, and wakens just that infinite longing which is the essence of romanticism. He is accordingly a completely romantic composer, and is not this perhaps the reason why he has less success with vocal music, which excludes the character of indefinite longing, merely representing emotions defined by words as emotions experienced in the realm of the infinite?

The musical rabble is oppressed by Beethoven's powerful genius; it seeks in vain to oppose it. But knowing critics, looking about them with a superior air, assure us that we may take their word for it as men of great intellect and deep insight that, while the excellent Beethoven can scarcely be denied a very fertile and lively imagination, he does not know how to bridle it! Thus, they say, he no longer bothers at all to select or to shape his ideas, but, following the so-called daemonic method, he dashes everything off exactly as his ardently active imagination dictates it to him. Yet how does the matter stand if it is *your* feeble observation alone that the deep inner continuity of Beethoven's every composition eludes? If it is *your* fault alone that you do not understand the master's language as the initiated understand it, that the portals of the innermost sanctuary remain closed to you? The truth is that, as regards self-possession, Beethoven stands quite on a par with Haydn and Mozart and that, separating his ego from the inner realm of harmony, he rules over it as an absolute monarch. In Shakespeare, our knights of the aesthetic measuring-rod have often bewailed the utter lack of inner unity and inner continuity, although for those who look more deeply there springs forth, issuing from a single bud, a beautiful tree, with leaves, flowers, and fruit; thus, with Beethoven, it is only after a searching investigation of his instrumental music that the high self-possession inseparable from true genius and nourished by the study of the art stands revealed.

Can there be any work of Beethoven's that confirms all this to a higher degree than his indescribably profound, magnificent symphony in C minor? How this wonderful composition, in a climax that climbs on and on, leads the listener imperiously forward into the spirit world of the infinite! . . . No doubt the whole rushes like an ingenious rhapsody past many a man, but the soul of each thoughtful listener is assuredly stirred, deeply and intimately, by a feeling that is none other than that unutterable portenetous longing, and until the final chord —indeed, even in the moments that follow it—he will be powerless to step out of that wondrous spirit realm where grief and joy embrace him in the form of sound. The internal structure of the movements, their execution, their instrumentation, the way in which they follow one another—everything contributes to a single end; above all, it is the intimate inter-relationship among the themes that engenders that unity which alone has the power to hold the listener firmly in a single mood. This relationship is sometimes clear to the listener when he overhears it in the connecting of two movements or discovers it in the fundamental bass they have in common; a deeper relationship which does not reveal itself in this way speaks at other times only from mind to mind, and it is precisely this relationship that prevails between sections of the two Allegros and the Minuet and which imperiously proclaims the self-possession of the master's genius.

How deeply thy magnificent compositions for the piano have impressed themselves upon my soul, thou sublime master; how shallow and insignificant now all seems to me that is not thine, or by the gifted Mozart or that mighty genius, Sebastian Bach! With what joy I received thy seventieth work, the two glorious trios, for I knew full well that after a little practice I should soon hear them in truly splendid style. And in truth, this evening things went so well with me that even now, like a man who wanders in the mazes of a fantastic park, woven about with all manner of exotic trees and plants and marvelous flowers, and who is drawn further and further in, I am powerless to find my way out of the marvelous turns and windings of thy trios. The lovely siren voices of these movements of thine, resplendent in their many-hued variety, lure me on and on. The gifted lady who indeed honored me, Capellmeister Kreisler,[3] by playing today the first trio in such splendid style, the gifted lady before whose piano I still sit and write, has made me realize quite clearly that only what the mind produces calls for respect and that all else is out of place.

Just now I have repeated at the piano from memory certain striking transitions from the two trios.

How well the master has understood the specific character of the instrument and fostered it in the way best suited to it!

A simple but fruitful theme, songlike, susceptible to the most varied contrapuntal treatments, curtailments, and so forth, forms the basis of each movement; all remaining subsidiary themes and figures are intimately related to the main idea in such a way that the details all interweave, arranging themselves among the instruments in highest unity. Such is the structure of the whole, yet in this artful structure there alternate in restless flight the most marvelous pictures in which joy and grief, melancholy and ecstasy, come side by side or intermingled to the fore. Strange figures begin a merry dance, now floating off into a point of light, now splitting apart, flashing and sparkling, evading and pursuing one another in various combinations, and at the center of the spirit realm thus disclosed the intoxicated soul gives ear to the unfamiliar

[3] The eccentric, half-mad musician from whose literary remains Hoffmann pretends to have taken his "Kreisleriana." Schumann borrows the title of his Opus 16 from these sketches of Hoffmann's (published in two groups as a part of his *Fantasiestücke in Callot's Manier*).—*Transl.*

language and understands the most mysterious premonitions that have stirred it.

That composer alone has truly mastered the secrets of harmony who knows how, by their means, to work upon the human soul; for him, numerical proportions, which to the dull grammarian are no more than cold, lifeless problems in arithmetic, become magical compounds from which to conjure up a magic world.

Despite the good nature that prevails, especially in the first trio, not even excepting the melancholy Largo, Beethoven's genius is in the last analysis serious and solemn. It is as though the master thought that, in speaking of deep mysterious things—even when the spirit, intimately familiar with them, feels itself joyously and gladly uplifted—one may not use an ordinary language, only a sublime and glorious one; the dance of the priests of Isis can be only an exultant hymn. Where instrumental music is to produce its effect simply through itself as music and is by no means to serve a definite dramatic purpose, it must avoid all trivial facetiousness, all frivolous *lazzi*. A deep temperament seeks, for the intimations of that joy which, an import from an unknown land, more glorious and more beautiful than here in our constricted world, enkindles an inner, blissful life within our breasts, a higher expression than can be given to it by mere words, proper only to our circumscribed earthly air. This seriousness, in all of Beethoven's works for instruments and for the piano, is in itself enough to forbid all those breakneck passages up and down for the two hands which fill our piano music in the latest style, all the queer leaps, the farcical capriccios, the notes towering high above the staff of their five- and six-line scaffolds.

On the side of mere digital dexterity, Beethoven's compositions for the piano really present no special difficulty, for every player must be presumed to have in his fingers the few runs, triplet figures, and whatever else is called for; nevertheless, their performance is on the whole quite difficult. Many a so-called virtuoso condemns this music, objecting that it is "very difficult" and into the bargain "very ungrateful."

Now, as regards difficulty, the correct and fitting performance of a work of Beethoven's asks nothing more than that one should understand him, that one should enter deeply into his being, that—conscious of one's own consecration—one should boldly dare to step into the circle of the magical phenomena that his powerful spell has evoked. He who is not conscious of this consecration, who regards sacred Music as a mere game, as a mere entertainment for an idle hour, as a momentary stimulus for dull ears, or as a means of self-ostentation—let him leave Beethoven's music alone. Only to such a man, moreover, does the objection "most ungrateful" apply. The true artist lives only in the work that he has understood as the composer meant it and that he then performs. He is above putting his own personality forward in any way, and all his endeavors are directed toward a single end—that all the wonderful enchanting pictures and apparitions that the composer has sealed into his work with magic power may be called into active life, shining in a thousand colors, and that they may surround mankind in luminous sparkling circles and, enkindling its imagination, its innermost soul, may bear it in rapid flight into the faraway spirit realm of sound.[4]

[4] Hoffmann's essay was brought to Beethoven's attention in February or March 1820 by someone who wrote, during a conversation with him: "In the *Fantasiestücke* of Hoffmann there is much talk about you. Hoffmann used to be the music-director in Bromberg; now he is a state counsellor. They give operas by him in Berlin." On the strength of this, evidently, Beethoven wrote the following letter to Hoffmann on March 23, 1820:

Through Herr ———, I seize this opportunity of approaching a man of your intellectual attainments. You have even written about my humble self, and our Herr ——— showed me in his album some lines of yours about me. I must assume, then, that you take a certain interest in me. Permit me to say that, from a man like yourself, gifted with such distinguished qualities, this is very gratifying to me. I wish you the best of everything and remain, sir,

> Your devoted and respectful,
> Beethoven—*Transl.*

18

Hector Berlioz

1 8 0 3 - 1 8 6 9

THE ORCHESTRA

Composer, conductor, journalist, librarian, Hector Berlioz
typifies the many-sided artist of the Romantic era. Through his
music and his treatise on orchestration (the first of its kind)
he contributed greatly to the development of the modern symphony orchestra. This excerpt is from his *Mémoires,* compiled
from 1848 to 1854.

THE ORCHESTRA MAY BE considered a large instrument capable
of playing a great number of different tones simultaneously or
in succession. Its power is moderate or gigantic according to
the proportionate use of all or only part of the resources available to the modern orchestra, and according to the more or less
propitious application of these resources in relation to acoustic
conditions of various types.

The performers of all sorts, constituting together the orchestra, are, so to speak, its strings, tubes, pipes, sounding boards—
machines endowed with intelligence, but subject to the action
of an immense keyboard played by the conductor under the
direction of the composer.

The placing of the musicians is of great importance; whether
they are arranged on a horizontal or an inclined platform, in a
space enclosed on three sides, or in the middle of the hall;
whether there are reflectors and whether these have hard sur-
faces (throwing back the sound) or soft ones (absorbing and

breaking it); how close the reflectors are to the performers—all of this is of extraordinary consequence.

The best way of placing an orchestra in a hall sufficiently large for the number of players used is to arrange them in rows one above the other on a series of steps in such a fashion that each row can send its tones to the listener without any intervening obstacles. Every well-directed orchestra should thus be arranged in echelons. If it plays on the stage of the theater the scene should be enclosed by wooden walls in the rear, at the sides, and above.

In the past the number of string instruments in opera orchestras was always in correct proportion to that of the other instruments; but for some years this has no longer been the case. An orchestra which had only two flutes, two oboes, two clarinets, two French horns, two bassoons, rarely two trumpets, and hardly ever any kettledrums, was well-balanced with 9 first violins, 8 second violins, 6 violas, 7 violoncellos, and 6 doublebasses. The makeup of such an orchestra would be sufficient for the performance of Haydn's and Mozart's symphonies. Nowadays, however, with four horns, three trombones, two trumpets, a bass drum, and kettledrums, but still with the same number of string instruments, the balance is completely destroyed. The violins are scarcely audible and the total effect is extremely unsatisfactory. There should be at least 15 first violins, 14 second violins, 10 violas, and 12 violoncellos properly to project Beethoven's symphonies, von Weber's overtures, and more modern compositions in the monumental or passionate style.

By doubling or tripling the number of performers in the same proportion one could doubtless obtain a magnificent orchestra for a music festival. General prejudice charges large orchestras with being noisy. However, if they are well-balanced, well-rehearsed, and well-conducted, and if they perform truly good music, they should rather be called powerful. In fact, nothing is as different in meaning as these two expressions. Three trombones, if clumsily employed, may appear noisy and unbearable; the very next minute, in the same hall, twelve trombones will delight the listeners with their powerful and yet noble tone. In fact, unisons are effective only if executed by many instruments. Thus, four first-rate violinists playing the same part will produce a rather unpleasant effect, whereas fifteen average violinists in unison would sound excellent. This is why small orchestras are of so little effect and hence of so little value, however accomplished the performance of the individual players.

On the other hand, the thousand combinations possible with a giant orchestra could produce a wealth of harmonies, a variety of sounds, and abundance of contrasts surpassing anything heretofore achieved in art. It could create, above all, an incalculable melodic, rhythmic, and expressive power, a penetrating force of unparalleled strength, a miraculous sensitivity of gradations, in the whole or in any individual part. Its calm would be as majestic as an ocean in repose, its outbursts would recall tropical tempests, its explosive power the eruptions of volcanos. In it could be heard plaints, the murmurings, the mysterious sounds of primeval forests, the outcries, the prayers, the triumphant or mourning chants of a people with an expansive soul, an ardent heart, and fiery passions. Its silence would inspire awe by its solemnity. But its crescendo would make even the most unyielding listeners shudder, for it would grow like a tremendous conflagration gradually setting the sky on fire.

19

Donald Jay Grout

1902-

NATIONALISM, OLD AND NEW

NATIONALISM WAS AN important force in nineteenth-century music. A distinction must be made, however, between early Romantic nationalism and the nationalism which appeared after 1860. The results of the early nineteenth-century German folk song revival were so thoroughly absorbed into the fabric of German music as to become an integral part of its style, which in the Romantic period was the nearest thing to an international European musical style. In similar fashion, the national qualities of the nineteenth-century French and Italian music were assimilated to a firmly established tradition in each country

The new nationalism, in contrast to the old, flourished exclusively in countries that had no great or unbroken musical tradition of their own but had long been musically dependent on other nations, chiefly Germany. Nationalism was one of the weapons by which composers in those countries sought to free themselves from the domination of foreign music. As a movement, it was self-conscious, and sometimes aggressive. It underlies such externals as the choice of national subjects for operas and symphonic poems, the collecting and publishing of folk songs, and the occasional quoting of folk tunes in compositions; but a more important consequence was the rise of new styles through fertilization of orthodox Germanic music by tonal, melodic, harmonic, rhythmic, and formal characteristics of the national idioms. This development took place earliest in Russia.

Until well into the nineteenth century secular art music in Russia was exclusively in the hands of imported Italian, French, or German composers. The history of Russian music begins in 1836 with the performance of the patriotic opera *A Life for the Tsar* by Michael Glinka (1804-1857). Although nationalism was more evident in the libretto than in the music, this work gave impetus to a movement that gained momentum with Glinka's second opera, *Russlan and Ludmilla* (1842) and the operas *Russalka* (1856) and *The Stone Guest* (1867) by Alexander Dargomizhsky (1813-1869). The principal Russian nationalists were a group of composers known as "the Mighty Five": César Cui (1835-1918), Mily Balakirev (1837-1910), Alexander Borodin (1833-1887), Modest Mussorgsky (1839-1881), and Nicolas Rimsky-Korsakov (1844-1908).

In their fight to create an all-Russian style of music, the nationalist composers' comparative ignorance of conservatory harmony and counterpoint became a positive asset: it forced them to discover their own ways of doing things, and in the process they used the materials nearest at hand, namely folk songs. Their frequent use of actual or imitated folk material for the generating themes of a work "has literary parallels in the borrowing by Pushkin and Gogol of folk-tales as the bases of so many of their most characteristic stories."

Russian folk tunes tend to move within a narrow range and to be made up either of obsessive repetition of one or two rhythmic motives of phrases in irregular rhythm constantly sinking to a cadence, often by the interval of a descending fourth. Another prominent feature of Russian folk songs, and of Mussorgsky's melodies, is their modal character, and this modality affected Mussorgsky's harmonic style, as well as that of all the Russian nationalists. Brahms had used modal chords and progressions, but it was the Russians first of all who were responsible for introducing modality into the general musical language of Europe, and their influence in this respect on the music of the early twentieth century is important.

Bedřich Smetana and Anton Dvořák, the two principal Czech composers of the nineteenth century, have already been mentioned in connection with the symphonic and chamber music of the Romantic period. Bohemia had for centuries been an Austrian crown land, and thus, unlike Russia, had always been in contact with the main stream of European music; her folk songs do not differ from those of western nations nearly so much as the Russian. Nor was the Czech nationalist movement marked from the outset, as was the Russian, by self-conscious efforts to avoid western influence. The nationalism of Smetana and Dvořák is chiefly apparent in the choice of national subjects for program music and operas, and by an infusion of their basic musical language (Smetana's derived from Liszt, Dvořák's more like Brahms's) with a melodic freshness and spontaneity, a harmonic and formal nonchalance, together with occasional traces of folklike tunes and popular dance rhythms.

Nationalism in Norway is represented by Edvard Hagerup Grieg (1843-1907), whose best works are his short piano pieces, songs, and incidental orchestral music to plays. (The two suites that Grieg arranged from his music for Ibsen's Peer Gynt [1875, reorchestrated 1886] include only eight of the original twenty-three numbers.)

In Spain nationalist impetus came from the works of Isaac Albeniz, whose piano suite Iberia used Spanish dance rhythms in a colorful virtuoso style. The principal Spanish composer of the early twentieth century, Manuel de Falla, collected and arranged national folk songs, and his earlier works—for example, the opera La Vida breve (Life is Short) and the ballet El Amor Brujo (Love, the Sorcerer)—are imbued with the melodic and rhythmic qualities of Spanish popular music.

20

Vladimir Vassilievitch Stassov

1824-1906

NATIONALISM IN RUSSIAN MUSIC

V. V. Stassov, a Russian journalist, vigorously championed
Russian nationalism in his writings. He was one of the chief
spokesmen for the Russian National School. In 1883 he completed a history of *Russian Music During the Last 25 Years,*
from which the following excerpt is taken.

OUR NEW SCHOOL is characterized by another significant feature:
its striving for the national. This had already begun with
Glinka and continues without interruption until today. In no
other European school can such a striving be found. The historical and cultural presuppositions among other nations were
of such a character that long ago the folk song—the expression
of direct, original, popular musicality among the majority of
civilized peoples—had disappeared almost entirely. Who knows
and still hears French, German, Italian or English folk songs
in the nineteenth century? Naturally they were present and
were once in general use; but the levelling scythe of European
culture, which is so hostile to the original elements of life, has
descended upon them, and now the efforts of music archaeolo-
gists or inquisitive explorers are required to discover the fragments of ancient folk songs in remote corner of the provinces.
The situation is completely different in our motherland. The folk
song still resounds everywhere to this very day: every peasant,

every carpenter, every mason, every porter, every coachman, every old woman, every washer-woman, and every cook, every nurse, and every wet-nurse, bring it along with them from their homes to Petersburg, to Moscow, to every other city and one hears it the whole year through. It surrounds us always and everywhere. Every worker in Russia does his work while singing a whole series of songs just as has been done for thousands of years. The Russian soldier goes to battle with a folk song on his lips. This is known to all of us and no archaeological effort is needed to become acquainted with it and to love it. Therefore every Russian who comes to the world with a creative musical soul grows up from the first day of his life among musical elements which are basically national. Thus it has come about that almost all significant Russian musicians were born not in the capitals but in the interior of Russia, in provincial cities or on paternal estates and spent their first youth there (Glinka, Dargomyzhsky, Musorgsky, Balakirev, Rimski-Korsakov). Others spent not a few of their youthful years in the provinces outside the city in frequent and close contact with the folk song and folk singing. The first and original musical impressions were national ones. The reason why an artistically developed folk music did not exist in Russia earlier must be found exclusively in the unfavorable nature . . . But scarcely had the times changed a little, scarcely was there talk in life and literature about the national consciousness, scarcely were the inclinations for this aroused again, when immediately gifted people appeared who wished to create a type of music in popular Russian forms which lay closest to them and were dear to them. Without doubt European composers (at least the most powerful and the most gifted among them) would have trod the same path upon which our composers beginning with Glinka now go. This path, however, did not exist for them any more. This can be very clearly proven by the eagerness with which they always took up everything national in music, even foreign music, no matter how slight this might be. Let us recall how, for example, Beethoven attempted more than once to choose as themes Russian folk songs, Franz Schubert Slavic, Liszt Hungarian ones. Nevertheless they did not create Russian, Slavic or Hungarian music. Music does not consist merely of themes. To be national, to express the national spirit and the national soul, it must reach the very roots of popular life. But neither Beethoven nor Schubert nor Liszt ever turned to national life. They only took precious gems which had remained preserved among one or another people in order to place these beautiful, fresh, eternally young sparkling jewels into that musical setting which is characteristic of European art music in general. They did not plunge into that world which they had accidentally hit upon and to which these beautiful and characteristic fragments belonged. They only played with them, took delight in their beauty and represented them in the splendid illumination of their talent. Other conditions of life had fallen to the lot of the Russian masters. They are not strange guests in that world from which they drew our national and Slavic melodies. They are at home there and therefore they have the melodies at their disposal and are capable of presenting them in the entire truth and power of their coloring, their spiritual nature and character. What Glinka created is already generally known and generally recognized. He prepared the new path, he created the national opera in forms which exist nowhere in Europe. Glinka's successors followed in his footsteps and relied in this on his brilliant example and initiative.

In connection with the national Russian element there is something else which is characteristic of the new Russian trend in music. It is the Oriental element. Nowhere in Europe does it play such a prominent role as with our musicians. They shared in this regard the general Russian predilection for everything Oriental. . . . It is, therefore, no wonder when so much that is Oriental has again and again found entrance into the content of Russian life and all its forms and has given it such a particularly characteristic coloring. Already Glinka had felt this and therefore he said in his *Notes,* "Without doubt our Russian song is a child of the North, but the inhabitants of the East have also contributed a little to it." Just as in the case of Glinka many of his best works are full of the Oriental element, so too many of the best works of all his adherents and continuers are filled with them.

21

Richard Wagner

1813-1883

THE ART WORK OF THE FUTURE

Wagner's creation of the "music drama" is an attempt to
achieve musical and dramatic unity by having the music follow
the drama in its most minute details disregarding the formal
patterns of traditional opera. Richard Wagner devoted himself
almost exclusively to opera and music drama as a composer and
writer. The present excerpt is from *The Art Work of the Future*
(1850).

IF WE CONSIDER the situation of modern art—insofar as it is
actually *art*—in relation to public life, we recognize first of all
its complete inability to influence this public life in accordance
with its high purpose. This is because, as a mere cultural
product, it has not grown out of life, and because, as a hot-
house plant, it cannot possibly take root in the natural soil
and natural climate of the present. Art has become the exclusive
property of an artist class; it gives pleasure only to those who
understand it, requiring for its understanding a special study,
remote from real life, the study of *art connoisseurship*. This
study and the understanding it affords are thought today to
be within the reach of everyone who has the money to pay
for the art pleasures offered for sale; yet if we ask the artist
whether the great multitude of our art amateurs are capable of
understanding him in his highest flights, he can answer only

with a deep sigh. And if he now reflects on the infinitely greater multitude of those who must remain cut off, as a result of the influence of our social conditions, unfavorable from every point of view, not only from the understanding, but even from the enjoyment of modern art, the artist of today cannot but become conscious that his whole artistic activity is, strictly speaking, only an egoistic self-complacent activity for activity's sake and that, in its relation to public life, his art is mere luxury, superfluity, and selfish pastime. The disparity, daily observed and bitterly deplored, between so-called culture and the lack of it is so monstrous, a mean between them so unthinkable, their reconciliation so impossible, that, granted a minimum of honesty, the modern art based on this unnatural culture would have to admit, to its deepest shame, that it owed its existence to a life element which in turn could base *its* existence only on the utter lack of culture in the real mass of humanity. The one thing that, in this, its alloted situation, modern art should be able to do—and, where there is honesty, does endeavor to do—namely, *to further the diffusion of culture* —it cannot do, for the simple reason that art, to have any influence on life, must be itself the flowering of a *natural* culture—that is, of one that has grown up from below—and can never be in a position to rain down culture from above. At best, then, our cultured art resembles the speaker who seeks to communicate with a people in a language which it does not understand—all that he says, his most ingenious sayings above all, can lead only to the most laughable confusions and misunderstandings.

Let us first make apparent how modern art is to proceed if it would attain *theoretically* to the redemption of its uncomprehended self from out its isolated situation and to the widest possible understanding of the public; how this redemption can become possible only through the *practical* mediation of the public will then be readily apparent of itself.

Man as artist can be fully satisfied only in the union of all the art varieties in the *collective* art work; in every *individualization* of his artistic capacities he is *unfree*, not wholly that which he can be; in the collective art work he is *free*, wholly that which he can be.

The *true* aim of art is accordingly *all-embracing*; everyone animated by the true artistic impulses seeks to attain, through the full development of his particular capacity, not the glorification of *this particular capacity*, but the glorification *in art of mankind in general*.

The highest collective art work is the *drama*; it is present in its *ultimate completeness* only when *each art variety, in its ultimate completeness*, is present in it.

True drama can be conceived only as resulting from the *collective impulse of all the arts* to communicate in the most immediate way with a *collective public*; each individual art variety can reveal itself as *fully understandable* to this collective public only through collective communication, together with the other art varieties, in the drama, for the aim of each individual art variety is fully attained only in the mutually understanding and understandable co-operation of all the art varieties.

Not *one* of the richly developed capacities of the individual arts will remain unused in the collective art work of the future; it is precisely in the collective art work that these capacities will attain to full stature. Thus especially the art of tone, developed with such singular diversity in instrumental music, will realize in the collective art work its richest potentialities—will indeed incite the pantomimic art of dancing in turn to wholly new discoveries and inspire the breath of poetry no less to an undreamed-of fullness. For in its isolation, music has formed itself an organ capable of the most immeasurable expression—the *orchestra*. Beethoven's tonal language, introduced through the orchestra into the drama, is a force wholly new to the dramatic art work. If architecture and, still more so, scenic landscape painting can place the dramatic actor in the natural environment of the physical world and give him, from the inexhaustible font of natural phenomena, a background constantly rich and relevant, the orchestra—that animate body of infinite harmonic variety—offers the individual actor, as a support, what may be called a perpetual source of the natural element of man as artist. The orchestra is, so to speak, the soil of infinite universal feeling from which the individual feeling of the single actor springs into full bloom; it somehow dissolves the solid motionless floor of the actual scene into a fluid, pliant, yielding, impressionable, ethereal surface whose unfathomed bottom is the sea of feeling itself. Thus the orchestra resembles the *earth,* from which *Antaeus,* once he touched it with his feet, gathered renewed and deathless vital energy. Although by nature diametrically opposed to the actor's natural scenic environment and hence, as local color, placed very rightly in the deepened foreground outside the scenic frame, it also constitutes the perfect complement of scenic environment, expanding the inexhaustible natural element of the *physical* world to the no less inexhaustible emotional element of *man* as artist; this composite element encircles the actor as with an atmospheric elemental ring of nature and of art; in this he moves assured, as do the heavenly bodies, in ultimate completeness, at the same time sending forth in all directions his views and feelings, endlessly expanded, as do the heavenly bodies their rays, into the infinite distances.

Thus completing one another in their ever-changing round, the united sister arts will show themselves and bring their influence to bear, now collectively, now two at a time, now singly, as called for by the need of the dramatic action, the one determinant of aim and measure. At one moment plastic pantomime will listen to thought's dispassionate appraisal; at another the will of resolute thought will overflow into the

139

immediate expression of gesture; at still another music will have to utter the flood of feeling, the awe of apprehension; finally, however, all three, in mutual entwinement, will exalt the will of drama to immediate active deed. For there is one thing which all three united art varieties must will, would they be free to act —this is the *drama;* all three must be concerned for the attainment of the dramatic aim. If they are conscious of this aim, if all direct their will to its accomplishment, each will receive the strength to lop off on all sides the egoistic offshoots of its particular nature from the common trunk, in order that the tree may grow, not shapelessly in all directions, but to the proud summit of its branches, twigs, and leaves—to its crown.

Human nature, like the art variety, is in itself multiform and many-sided; the soul of the *individual* man—the activity most necessary to him, his strongest instinctive urge—is a *single* thing. If he recognizes this single thing as his basic nature, he can, to further its indispensable attainment, suppress each weaker, subordinate desire, each feeble longing whose satisfaction might hinder him in this attainment. Only the weak and impotent man discovers in himself no supremely strong and necessary soul's desire; at every moment he is subject to chance appetite, stirred up incidentally from without; precisely because this is mere appetite, he can never satisfy it; tossed willfully back and forth from one appetite to another, he never even attains to real enjoyment. But if this man, knowing no need, has might enough obstinately to pursue the satisfaction of these chance appetites, then there arise in life and art those horrible and monstrous phenomena which—as excrescences of mad egoistic impulses, as murderous debaucheries of despots, or as lascivious modern operas—fill us with such unspeakable disgust. If, on the other hand, the individual man discovers in himself a strong desire, an urge repressing every other longing that he feels, in other words, that necessary inner impulse which makes up his soul and being, and if he bends all his energy to satisfy it, then he exalts his might, and with it his particular capacity, to a strength and height he cannot otherwise attain.

The individual man, given perfect health of body, heart, and mind, can experience no higher need than that common to all men similarly constituted, for, as a *real* need, it can only be such as he can satisfy in the community alone. But the strongest and most necessary need of the perfect artist is to communicate himself in the ultimate completeness of his being to the ultimate community, and he attains this with the universal intelligibility necessary to it only in the *drama*. In the drama he expands his particular being to general being by representing an individual personality other than his own. He must wholly forget himself to comprehend another personality with the completeness necessary to representation; he attains this only when he explores this individuality with such precision in its contact, penetration, and completion with and by other individualities—hence also the being of these other individualities themselves—when he apprehends this individuality so accurately that it is possible for him to become conscious of this contact, penetration, and completion in his own being; the perfect representative artist is therefore the individual expanded to the *being of the species* in accordance with the ultimate completion of his own particular being. The scene in which this wondrous process is accomplished is the *theatrical stage;* the collective art work which it brings to light is the *drama*. To force his particular being to the highest flowering of its content in this *one* highest art work, the individual artist, however, like the individual art variety, has to repress each willful egoistic inclination to untimely expansion useless to the whole in order to be able to contribute the more actively to the attainment of the highest collective aim, which is in turn not to be realized without the individual and his periodic limitation.

This aim—the aim of the drama—is at the same time the

only genuinely artistic aim that can be possibly *realized;* whatever is remote from it must necessarily lose itself in the sea of the uncertain, the unintelligible, the unfree. And this aim is attained, not by *one art variety for itself alone,* but only by *all collectively,* and therefore the *most universal* art work is at the same time the one art work that is real and free—in other words, universally *intelligible.*

22

Donald Jay Grout

1902-

DEBUSSY AND IMPRESSIONISM

THE MOST CONSPICUOUS and influential development in French music in the late nineteenth and early twentieth centuries is incarnate in a single composer, Claude-Achille Debussy (1862-1918). *Impressionism* is a term that was first applied to a school of French painting which flourished from about 1880 to the end of the century; its chief representative is Claude Monet (1840-1926). In relation to music, the word is thus defined in Webster's Dictionary: "A style of composition designed to create descriptive impressions by evoking moods through rich and varied harmonics and timbres." Impressionism is thus a kind of program music. It differs from most Romantic program music in that, first, it does not seek to express feeling or tell a story, but to evoke a mood, an "atmosphere," with the help of suggestive titles and occasional reminiscences of natural sounds, dance rhythms, characteristic bits of melody, and the like; second, impressionism relies on allusion and understatement instead of the more forthright or strenuous methods of the Romantics; and third, it employs melodies, harmonies, colors, rhythms, and formal principles which, in their totality, make a musical language sharply different from that of the German Romantic tradition [which was overwhelmingly predominant at the time].

The chief element in that language is color: color not only in the narrow sense of timbre, but in the broader sense as rising from harmonic, melodic, and rhythmic factors as well. Melodies are likely to be short motives of narrow range, freely combined to make a musical mosaic of irregular, varicolored pieces. Pentatonic, whole-tone, [and other exotic] scales may furnish the material of melodies and chords. Rhythm, in the kind of music one most often thinks of as "impressionistic," is nonpulsatile, vague, concealed by syncopations and irregular subdivisions of the beat; but in some compositions by Debussy, the rhythm is a rapid, animated pulsation (often continued in ostinato fashion), or is patterned on some exotic or imagined dance. Outlines of phrases and the formal structure as a whole are deliberately blurred and indistinct, though in many impressionistic pieces a general three-part (*ABA*) form is discernible.

The principal means by which Debussy achieved his impressionistic color effects was harmony. One basic factor in his harmonic idiom is the use of chords in a largely "nonfunctional" manner: that is, chords are not used to shape a phrase by tension and release through a conventional series of progressions and resolutions; instead, each chord is conceived as a sonorous unit in a phrase whose structure is determined more by melodic shape or color value than by the movement of the harmony. Such a procedure does not negate tonality, which indeed Debussy was careful to preserve by pedal points or periodic frequent returns to the primary chords of the key; but the tonal relationships within the phrase may be so complex or willful that it is impossible to hear a given chord or series of chords as being in the key of the phrase in which they occur. The structure of chords is also veiled by abundance of figuration and, in the piano works, by the blending of sounds with the use of the damper pedal. A very common device is a succession of chords with parallel movement of all the voices.

Debussy's orchestration, like his piano writing, is admirably suited to the musical ideas. A large orchestra is required, but it is seldom used to make a loud sound. Strings are frequently divided and muted; harps add a distinctive touch; among the woodwinds, the flute (especially in the low register), oboe, and English horn are featured in solos; horns and trumpets, also often muted, are heard in short pianissimo phrases; percussion of many types—kettledrums, large and small drums, large and small cymbals, tam-tams, celesta, glockenspiel, xylophone—is still another source of color. With this music an enchanted world seems to rise before us—far-off, antique, misty with distance or bright with the unreal colors of a vision.

Debussy's national bent for musical exoticism was strengthened when he heard a Javanese *gamelan* orchestra at the Paris exposition in 1889, and it may be that his imaginative use of percussion and the many gong effects in his piano pieces were consequences of this experience.

The impressionism of Debussy is best regarded as a late and very special offshoot of Romanticism, shaped by French ideals but embodying the Romantic predilection for mood, color, and harmonic opulence in a homophonic texture with relaxed treatment of rhythm and form. Nevertheless the changes that Debussy introduced, particularly those in the harmonic system, link him with a later epoch. His work is distinctly a bridge between Classical and twentieth-century conceptions of tonality. Moreover, even though impressionism itself did not become a school, its effects were felt everywhere. To name the composers who at one time or another came under the influence of Debussy would be to name nearly every composer of the early twentieth century.

THE MODERN ERA

23

Joseph Machlis

1906-

THE MATERIALS OF CONTEMPORARY MUSIC

Joseph Machlis is Professor of Music at Queens College of
the University of the City of New York. Among his writings is
Introduction to Contemporary Music (1961), from which the
following selections were taken.

Introduction

ONE THING IN HISTORY never changes, and that is the element of
change itself. True, men always resist the unfamiliar. But the
dynamism of life forces them on to ever new perspectives and
new solutions. The story of mankind is the story of a continual
becoming, a ceaseless adventure whose frontiers ever widen.

What does change, from one age to the next, is the rate
of change. Certain periods are comparatively stable. The
force of tradition is strong, and acts to brake the new modes of
thought that are struggling to be born. At other times society
is in a state of flux. Horizons open up with breathtaking rapidity, and changes that in other epochs would be spread over
many generations are telescoped into a single lifetime. Ours is
such an era. Today the rate of change, both social and cultural, has been enormously accelerated. Life demands from us

signal powers of adjustment if we are not to be left behind.

Music, one of the major manifestations of man's creative impulse, has changed constantly through the ages, as every living language must. Each generation of musicians inherits a tradition, an established body of usages and techniques which it enriches by its own efforts and passes on to the next generation. At three points in the history of music—as it happens, they were equally distant from each other—the forces of change were so much in the ascendant that the word *new* became a battle cry. Around the year 1300 progressive composers were referred to as *moderni* and their art designated as *ars nova,* "New Art." The breakthrough of this modernism produced new rhythmic and harmonic principles as well as basic reforms in notation. The year 1600 is another such landmark. The contemporaries of Monteverdi raised the banner of *le nuove musiche,* "The New Music"; expressive melody and the dramatic concept of opera challenged the tradition of religious choral music. Similarly, around 1900 there emerged the New Music, with an explosiveness that gave rise to many a bitter battle. . . .

The new is born from the old and retains certain features of the old. In the heat of battle the new may seem like the ruthless destroyer of the old; but when the tumult subsides its innovations stand revealed as the inevitable continuation of the past. In the early years of this century audiences were persuaded that the art of music as they had known it was coming to an end, and responded accordingly. Perfectly respectable individuals in Paris and Vienna hissed and hooted, banged chairs, and engaged in fisticuffs with strangers. Less than half a century later, the works that caused these antics are enthroned as classics of the modern repertory. The men who wrote them are acknowledged masters; their disciples occupy key positions in our conservatories and colleges. The techniques and procedures once regarded as startling have become part of the accepted vocabulary of musical art. Although we like to think that human nature never changes, actually we are more adaptable than we suspect. Music that bewildered and jarred the listeners of fifty years ago is today heard by a rapidly growing public with every evidence of pleasure.

We are still too close to this great upheaval to be able to pass final judgment upon it. Yet, now that more than half our century is over, we can begin to view the New Music with some measure of perspective, and see that what at first appeared to be a violent revolution was in reality a necessary evolution. Significantly, the leaders of the modern movement disclaimed revolutionary intent. "I hold that it was error," Igor Stravinsky wrote, "to regard me as a revolutionary. If one only need break habit in order to be labeled a revolutionary, then every artist who has something to say and who in order to say it steps outside the bounds of established convention could be considered revolutionary." And Arnold Schoenberg to the same point: "I personally hate to be called a revolutionary, which I am not. What I did was neither revolution nor anarchy."

These statements attest to what every artist knows: that rules are not broken for the sheer joy of breaking them. For the artist, as for the philosopher, there is no absolute freedom, only freedom as "the recognition of necessity." The artist accepts the necessity of rules just as boys do when they play baseball, and for the same reason: to achieve freedom of action within a self-imposed frame. If he discards the inherited rules it is only because they have ceased to be meaningful—that is, fruitful—for him. He rejects them only so that he may impose other rules upon himself. In short, the rules change, but not the concept of rule, the eternal principle of law and order which is basic to the discipline of art.

When the New Music was first heard, people asked why composers could not go on writing like Tchaikovsky or Puccini.

The answer is obvious. Art, as an integral part of life, has to change just as life itself changes. The melodies of Tchaikovsky and Puccini were part of the nineteenth-century world. Stravinsky, Schoenberg, Bartók, and their contemporaries no longer inhabited that world. They had perforce to move on, to discover melodies that would express the present as eloquently as those of the masters had expressed the past. . . .

We use the term *modern*, as we do Baroque, Classical, or Romantic, to describe events of a certain period in time. Yet it would be wiser to avoid drawing hard and fast boundaries around the art of a period that is still in a state of flux. Besides, every generation has its own concept of what is modern. In general, we use *modern, new, twentieth-century* and *contemporary* as though they were interchangeable. Yet are they? *Contemporary*, strictly speaking, is a chronological designation that refers to anything happening in our time. But not everything that is contemporary is modern. For example, Rachmaninov and Gretchaninov were contemporary with Stravinsky, Schoenberg, and Bartók. They all lived in the twentieth century; yet they most certainly differed in regard to the degree of modernity in their work.

Within the range of contemporary music are composers who are ultra-conservative and those who are ultra-radical, with all manner of middle-of-the-roaders between. It is neither necessary nor possible to find a label that will cover both Sibelius and Anton Webern, both Menotti and Karlheinz Stockhausen. In this book, therefore, we will use *contemporary* in its broadest sense as synonymous with twentieth-century music, taking as our point of departure the beginning of our century. *"New Music"* is a narrower term, and is used here to refer to the styles that emerged immediately before and after the first World War.

There was a time when books on modern music appealed to the reader to rid himself of his prejudices and to approach the subject with an open mind. Such exhortations are no longer necessary. We live in twentieth-century houses, we wear twentieth-century clothes, and we think twentieth-century ideas. Why then should we shut ourselves off from twentieth-century music? Only those who fear the present aspire to live in the long ago. They gaze so fixedly toward the past that, in the memorable phrase of H. G. Wells, they walk into the future backwards. Let us rather lay ourselves open to all music, savoring the best of the old along with the new. In the process we shall vastly enrich our understanding of both.

A Review of the Romantic and Classical Eras

A work of art exists on two levels. On the one hand it embodies a deeply felt experience, a moment of rapturous awareness projected by a creative temperament. On the other, it embodies a way of shaping sensuous material—sounds, colors, blocks of marble, words—into artistic forms, according to techniques and procedures that derive from the nature of that material. In other words, a work of art possesses an expressive content and a formal content.

Form and content are indivisible parts of the whole. They can no more be separated than can body and mind. However, the emphasis may rest upon the one or the other. We call that attitude *classical* which seeks above all to safeguard the purity of form. We call that attitude *romantic* which concerns itself primarily with the expression of emotion.

The classicist exalts the values of order, lucidity, restraint. He seeks purity of style and harmonious proportion, striving to bring to perfection what already exists rather than to originate new forms. Achieving a certain measure of detachment from the art work, he expresses himself through symbols that have a universal validity. The romanticist, on the other hand, exalts the unique character of his personal reactions and strives al-

153

ways for the most direct expression of his emotions. He rebels against tradition, valuing passionate utterance above perfection of form. He sees the strangeness and wonder of life. His is an art of infinite yearning, rich in mood and atmosphere, picturesque detail, and striking color. Music for him is an enchantment of the senses, an outpouring of the heart.

Classic and romantic correspond to two fundamental impulses in man's nature: classicism to his love of traditional standards, his desire that emotion be purged and controlled within a form, romanticism to his longing for the unattainable, his need for ecstasy and intoxication. Both impulses have asserted themselves throughout the history of art. There have been times however, when one markedly predominanted over the other. One such era was the nineteenth century, which has come to be called the age of romanticism.

The Romantic Era

The French Revolution signalized the birth of a new society which glorified the individual as never before. Freedom was its watchword: freedom of religion, freedom of enterprise, political and personal freedom. On the artistic front this need for untrammeled individualism took shape in the romantic movement. The romantic spirit pervaded the arts of poetry and painting, as is amply attested by the works of Keats and Shelley, Delacroix, Turner and their contemporaries. But it was in music that romanticism found its ideal expression: music, the art of elusive meanings and indefinable moods.

The nineteenth-century climate was hospitable to the belief that the prime function of music is to express emotion. The short lyric forms—art song and piano piece—came to the fore, incarnating all the youthful exuberance of the romantic movement. Schubert, Schumann, and Mendelssohn, Chopin, Liszt, and Brahms carried this appealing genre to its finest flower, finding the romantic song and piano piece ideal for subjective lyricism and intimate communication with the listener.

At the same time the nineteenth century was drawn to the spectacular and the grandiose. Having inherited the symphony from Beethoven, the romantic composers transformed it into a vehicle for purple rhetoric and dramatic gesture—two elements dear to the age of Byron and Victor Hugo. Theirs was a music of sumptuous color and shattering climaxes, rich in poetic utterance, based upon the sonorous magic of the orchestra. Berlioz, Wagner, and Liszt were the leading proponents of what they boldly called "the Music of the Future." They perfected the genre of program music—that is to say, of music associated with specific literary or pictorial images—in which a poetic idea assumed a central position within the expressive scheme. In so doing they established music as a language of symbols, as the expression of literary-philosophical, world-encompassing ideas that must actuate all mankind. Program music was as basic to the nineteenth century as "pure" or absolute music was to the classically minded eighteenth. Why? Because to the romantic composer music was more than a manipulation of themes, harmonies, rhythms. To him, the sounds were inseparably allied with feelings about life and death, love and longing, God, nature, man defying his fate. To return to the terminology of the beginning of this chapter, the romantic musician valued the expressive content of music more than he did its purely formal content.

The central figure in the nineteenth-century ferment was Richard Wagner (1813-1883), whose grandiose dramas best exemplify the German penchant for attaching "deep" meanings to music. Nature and intuition are glorified in his operas, which hymn German forest and mountain, the Rhine, the ancient Teutonic myths of gods and heroes; which sing of love and passion with an abandon never before achieved; and in which, in *The Ring of the Nibelung,* the proceedings on stage are infused with all manner of political, moral and philosophical symbols. Wagner expressed the typically romantic desire for a "union of the arts." If music, poetry, and painting could produce such moving effects separately, how much greater would be their impact if they were combined? He was persuaded that only in his theater would all the arts find their mutual fulfillment: music, poetry, and drama, dance, painting (scenery), and sculpture (the plastic movements and poses of the actors). Through his use of *Leitmotives* or "guiding motives"—compact themes which symbolize characters, emotion, ideas, and even objects in his dramas—he brought to its farthermost limits the romantic attempts to make music conjure up specific images and feelings. Wagner's harmonic procedures, we shall see, had decisive importance for those who came after him. *Tristan and Isolde* heralds the impending crises in romanticism, in harmonic language, and in the whole system of assumptions on which western music was based.

A classicist strain in romanticism was exemplified in the early part of the century by Mendelssohn, in the latter part by Brahms. These two composers were quite different from one another; and they differed even more from a musician like Verdi. Yet all three had in common a horror of philosophical disquisitions in music, and a desire to make their art function on a purely abstract level of expressivity. The most vociferous exponent of this classical point of view was the critic Eduard Hanslick (1825-1904). He is remembered today chiefly as the prototype of Beckmesser, Wagner's savage caricature of a hidebound pedant in *Die Meistersinger.* Actually, Hanslick was an able thinker who disliked Wagner's ideas rather than his music. He was irreconcilably opposed to the extramusical trend of the "Music of the Future." And he enthusiastically supported the attempts of his friend Brahms to lead music back to the purity of the absolute forms—to the symphony and sonata which the nineteenth century had inherited from the eighteenth. . . .

The Classical Era

The Classical period in music extended through the half century that preceded the romantic. It reached its high point with the masters of the Viennese school—Haydn, Mozart, Beethoven, and Schubert.

The Classical era witnessed the American and French revolutions, as well as the English movement for political reform. These countries passed from absolute monarchy to a system based on political democracy and capitalist technology. The art of the Classical period reflects the unique movement in history when the old order was dying and the new was in process of being born; when the elegance of the aristocratic tradition met the vigor and humanism of a rising middle-class culture. Out of this climate emerged the grand form in both literature and music: the novel and the symphony, both destined to be vehicles of communication with a larger audience than had ever existed before.

The eighteenth-century artist functioned under the system of aristocratic patronage. He was attached to the household of a nobleman; he was employed by a municipal council or church; or he was commissioned to write a work for an opera house. In any case he produced for immediate use and was in direct contact with his public. He was a craftsman functioning in a handicraft society, creating beauty according to the accepted precepts of his time (although on occasion he chose to transcend those precepts). His public consisted of connoisseurs who were familiar with his medium by virtue of their birth. For so fastidious an audience he could be as painstaking and as subtle as he pleased.

The concept of art as self-expression was clearly not part of this environment. The artist created because he had the gift, and because the world in which he lived was eager for his product. He was far less concerned than his romantic successor with problems of esthetics and artistic inspiration, or with the opinion of posterity. Indeed, posterity was largely a nineteenth-century invention. The eighteenth-century artist created for a public high above him in social rank, who were intertested in his work rather than in him as an individual. To be personal in such circumstances would have been something of an impertinence. As a result, he was impelled to classical objectivity and reserve rather than to romantic revelation of self. The art of the Classical era bears the imprint of the spacious palaces that were its setting. In this milieu, emotional restraint was a prerequisite of good manners; impeccable taste was prized above all.

Alien to this world, also, was the Romantic concept of art as enchantment and dream. The Classical era regarded music as a necessary adornment of gracious living. The eighteenth-century composer constructed a piece for people to sing or play, to dance to or listen to as an agreeable pastime; this accounts for the prevailing good humor of so many classical works, in contrast to the sense of the tragic that pervades the art of the Romantic era. The Classical composer took for granted the power of music to express emotion; he therefore did not feel it necessary constantly to emphasize this aspect of his art, as did the romantic. He directed his attention rather to craftsmanship, beauty of design, and purity of style. Ecstasy and intoxication were alike foreign to his intent. Consequently he never strove for the "strangeness and wonder" of the romantics. Instead, he achieved the ideal balance between the need for expression and the control of form. There resulted an urbane art that continues to appeal, in the words of John Burroughs, to "our sense of the finely carved, the highly wrought, the deftly planned."

The Classical sonata-symphony was a spacious form allowing

for the expansion and development of abstract musical ideas.
. . . True, these themes had expressive content and mood.
They might be vivacious or sorrowful, pathetic or humorous;
yet they remained wholly within the domain of absolute music.
The Classical symphony steered clear of personal revelation,
specific emotions, litery and pictorial associations. There is profound emotion in the late works of Haydn and Mozart, as in the
volcanic symphonism of Beethoven; but this emotion is contained within the form, lifted from the subjective to the universal, from the temporary to the enduring, through the order and
discipline of classical art.

The romantics tried to draw music close to poetry and painting; the classical masters conceived of music as an independent,
self-contained art. Romantic music glorified folk song and dance;
the music of the classical era issued from the culture of cities
and the sophisticated circles of the court (even if the popular
tone begins to assert itself, significantly, in the lively finales of
Haydn). Nineteenth-century music was intensely nationalist
in spirit; the music of the late eighteenth century spoke an
inter-European language deriving from two international art
forms—Italian opera and Viennese symphony. For the romanticist, color and harmony, melody and rhythm existed as
values in themselves. The classicist subordinated all of these to
the over-all unity of the form: form as the principle of law and
order in art, born from the ideal mating of reason and emotion. It is this surpassing oneness of form and content that
constitutes the truly classical element in late eighteenth-century
music.

Nietzsche distinguished the classic from the romantic by
two vivid symbols: he opposed Apollo, god of light and harmonious proportion, to Dionysus, god of wine and intoxication.
The shift from the Dionysian principle to the Apollonian, as
we shall see, became the first decisive gesture of the New
Music. . . .

Melody

Contemporary composers do not emulate either the formal beauty of classical melody or the lyric expansiveness of the romantics. They range far afield for models, from the plasticity of Gregorian chant, the subtle irregularities of Medieval and Renaissance music, to the luxuriance of Bach's melodic line. Or, looking beyond the orbit of European music, they aspire to capture for the west the freedom, the improvisational quality of oriental melody.

The contemporary composer is not inclined to shape his melody to standardized patterns of four or eight bars. He does not eke out a phrase to four or eight measures solely because the preceding phrase was that long. He states a thing once, rather than two or three times. By abandoning symmetry and repetition he hopes to achieve a vibrant, taut melody from which everything superfluous has been excised. His aim is a finely molded, sensitive line packed with thought and feeling, which will function at maximum intensity as it follows the rise and fall of the musical impulse. Such a melody makes greater demands upon us than did the old. It requires alertness of mind and unflagging attention on the part of the listener, for its clipped phrases do not yield their meaning readily.

If the contemporary composer does adhere to traditional patterns, he uses them with all the subtlety at his command. Cadences are slurred over, phrases do not rhyme; punctuation marks are not made too perceptible. Repetitions are compressed, departure and return are veiled. As a matter of fact, this condensation of thought is not limited to music. Compare, for example, the rolling sentences of Dickens or Thackeray with the sinewy prose of Hemingway or Steinbeck; or the impassioned rhetoric of Shelley with the terse, wiry utterance of contemporary poets. The melodies of Mozart, Schubert, Chopin, and Tchaikovsky were shaped to the curve of the human voice, even when written for instruments. This is why the instrumental themes of these masters can be converted, year after year, into popular song hits. Twentieth-century music, on the other hand, has detached instrumental melody from its vocal origins. The new melody is neither unvocal nor antivocal; it is simply not conceived in terms of what the voice can do. The themes of twentieth-century works contain wide leaps and jagged turns of phrase that are not to be negotiated vocally. Contemporary melody ranges through musical space, striding forward boldly along untrodden paths. Instinct with energy and force, its line is apt to be angular rather than curved.

In addition, contemporary melody does not unfold against a background of familiar chords and scales. It does not move in the rhythms that we have grown accustomed to. It does not gravitate to the central tone or keynote as obviously as it once did. In effect, it avoids many of the landmarks on which people rely to mark out a melody. This loss of conventional intelligibility, however, is made up for in strength and freshness of expression, and in the avoidance of all turns of phrase that had become stereotyped from overuse. In this fashion the melodic line has been revitalized and rendered capable of conveying the new meanings—twentieth-century meanings. . . .

We must remember that twentieth-century music embraces many styles, ranging from the solidly conservative to extreme radicalism. For this reason any generalization about present-day melody must be accompanied by all sorts of qualifications. One fact, however, is indisputable. The twentieth century recognizes the primacy of melody even as did the eighteenth and nineteenth. When people accuse modern music of having abandoned melody, what they really mean is that it has abandoned the familiar landmarks on which they rely to recognize melody. Once we have learned to dispose with the punctuation marks of the good old days—just as we do when we read a telegram—we will be ready to respond to the exciting new conceptions of melody that have evolved in our time. We will find that, today as in the past, melody has pointed out, "What survives every change of system is melody." . . .

Harmony

The history of the development of harmony, Schoenberg points out, is a record of dissonance rather than consonance, for dissonance is the dynamic element that leads the composer away from well trodden paths. By the same token, it is the element which in every age—whether Monteverdi's, Bach's, Wagner's, or our own—has acutely disturbed the adherents of the past. "Dissonances are more difficult to comprehend than consonance," Schoenberg observes. "Therefore the battle about them goes on throughout history."

This battle came to a head in the late nineteenth century. Wagner and his disciples assiduously explored the expressive powers of dissonance, and superimposed upon the classical system of harmony a network of relationships that completely changed the existing harmonic idiom. In so doing they enormously enriched the harmonic resources available to the composer, and set the stage for an exciting break with the past.

The twentieth century inherited chord structures of three, four, and five tones. Carrying the traditional method of building chords one step farther, twentieth-century composers added another "story" to the chord, thus forming highly dissonant combinations of six and seven tones—for instance, chords based on steps 1-3-5-7-9-11 and 1-3-5-7-9-11-13 of the scale. The emergence of these complex "skyscraper" chords imparted a greater degree of tension to music than had ever existed before. . . .

A seven-tone "skyscraper" is, in effect, a *polychord*. It is a block of sound that is heard on two or three planes. A succession of such chords creates several planes of harmony. One of the outstanding achievements of the new age is a kind of *polyharmony* in which the composer plays two or more streams of harmony against each other, exactly as in former times single strands of melody were combined. The interplay of the several independent streams adds a new dimension to the harmonic space. . . .

By the end of the nineteenth century many dissonances had become so familiar that the composer was ready to accept them as consonant. Twentieth-century music emancipated the dissonance—that is, freed it from the need to proceed to the resolving consonance. Now the composer could either sidestep or entirely omit progressions that had become too standardized, excising what was not absolutely essential to his thought. The new harmony, like the new melody, moved away from the expansiveness of the classic-romantic style. It was marked by utmost economy of means and condensation of thought: a taut, telegraphic style that avoided the obvious and often derived its power from the element of surprise.

Inevitably the contemporary composer has abandoned the time-honored distinction between consonance and dissonance. To him the consonance is not basically different from the dissonance; it is simply less dissonant. As Schoenberg formulates it, "Dissonances are only the more remote consonances." In other words, the distinction is relative rather than absolute. A chord is no longer held to be consonant because of its intrinsic character, but because it is less dissonant than the chords that preceded it. Which means that a greater dissonance may be resolved to a lesser as effectively as it once resolved to a consonance. . . .

By abandoning the classical distinction between consonance and dissonance, contemporary music has changed the nature of the harmonic cadence. Cadences are much less in evidence than they were formerly; they are veiled, elided, subtilized. The old punctuation marks have disappeared. Often a modern work will unfold without a single complete cadence in the course of it. This implies a much greater accumulation of tension, and it means that the structure is less clearly articulated than it used to be. The listener is expected to go for a much longer period without "coming up for air"; in other words, to absorb a greater stretch of music at a time.

Nineteenth-century music explored the possibilities of dissonant harmony for sensuous color, emotional expression, and sonorous enchantment. The new harmony, on the other hand, exploited the dissonance as a percussive clang, a jabbing thrust of sound capable of engendering tension. Thus came into being the muscular harmonies of the New Music: those steely "hammered" chords that introduced a new tone into twentieth-century style. . . .

In contemporary music, melody and harmony are no longer indivisible, as they were in the Classic-Romantic era. Twentieth-century melody sometimes moves irrespective of harmonic progressions, achieving a freedom undreamed of in former times. This melody is no longer conceived in relation to standard chord structures or bolstered by familiar harmonies. As often as not the skips in the melodic line imply harmonic groupings to which neither our ears nor our vocal cords are accustomed. If this absence of standardization allows for freshness and novelty, it also makes it more difficult for us to apprehend the melody—at any rate, until we have heard enough contemporary music to build up a body of memories and associations comparable to those which help us apprehend the traditional melodic patterns. . . .

Tonality

In their desire to free music from what Béla Bartók called

"the tyrannical rule of the major-minor keys," twentieth-century composers found their way to broader notions of tonality. One of the most fruitful of the new concepts involves the free use of twelve tones around a center. This retains the basic principle of traditional tonality, loyalty to the Tonic; but, by considering the five chromatic tones to be as much a part of the key as the seven diatonic ones, it immeasurably expands the borders of tonality. In other words, the chromatic scale of seven basic tones and five visitors has given way to a duodecuple scale of twelve equal members.

This expanded conception of tonality has not only done away with the distinction between diatonic and chromatic, but also wiped out the distinction between major and minor that was so potent a source of contrast in the Classic-Romantic era. The composers of the eighteenth and nineteenth centuries presented them simultaneously. A piece today will be, let us say, in F major-minor, using all the twelve tones around the center F, instead of dividing them, as was done in the past, into two separate groups of seven. This serves to create an ambiguous tonality which is highly congenial to the taste of our time.

In general, the key is no longer so clearly defined an area in musical space as it used to be, and the shift from one key center to another is made with a dispatch that puts to shame the most exuberant modulations of the Wagner era. Transitional passages are dispensed with. One tonality is simply displaced by another, in a way that keeps both the music and the listener on the move. . . . Composers such as Stravinsky and Hindemith were leaders in the attempt to broaden the traditional concept of loyalty to the Tonic and to free contemporary music from a frame of reference that had become restrictive. . . .

Desirous of exploiting new harmonic resources, composers found inspiration in the exotic scales of China, India, Java, and other far-eastern countries. They also turned to the ancient scales embodied in European folk music, to the music of the

Middle Ages and Renaissance, to the medieval scale patterns called the church modes, and they began to experiment with the construction of new scales.

Tonality implies the supremacy of a single key and a single tone center. Composers in the past made the most out of the contrast between two keys heard in succession. Modern composers heighten the contrast by presenting them simultaneously.

The simultaneous use of two keys (*bitonality*) and of several (*polytonality*) came to the fore in the music of Stravinsky and Milhaud, whence it entered the vocabulary of the age. Toward the end of a polytonal piece, one key is generally permitted to assert itself over the others, and in this way an impression is restored of orderly progression toward a central point. Polytonality is used to bring out the different planes of the harmony. By putting two or more streams of chords in different keys the friction between them is immeasurably heightened. Piano music especially lends itself to the technique, right and left hands playing progressions of chords in different keys. Because the tension comes from the clash of keys, each stream of harmony must be rooted solidly in its own key. Polytonality, then, does not reject the principle of key. It merely extends this principle in a characteristically twentieth-century manner.

During the Twenties, Milhaud and his fellow experimenters were fond of combining three, four, or even five tonalities. However, it soon became apparent that most listeners are incapable of assimilating more than two keys at once with any degree of awareness. When three or more keys are combined the music tends to blur into dissonant passages that belong to no key at all. As a result, in recent years composers have written far less music in the polytonal idiom. Bitonality, on the other hand, has remained a most effective procedure in contemporary music. . . .

Rhythm

Musical rhythm presents varying degrees of organization. At one extreme is the regular beat of a Sousa march or a folk dance, so obvious as to be unmistakable. At the other are the freely flowing arabesques of oriental song, or of Gregorian chant, or of operatic recitative. These are the musical equivalents of free-verse and poetic-prose rhythms. Their rhythmic impulse comes from speech rather than from the symmetries of the dance.

The trend in western music from 1600 to 1900 was steadily in the direction of tighter organization—that is to say, toward metrical rhythm. There were several reasons for this. To begin with, European music was influenced in ever greater degree by folk dance and folk song, both of which were allied to popular metrical poetry. Then again, as the various literatures of Europe developed highly organized metrical verse forms, these could not but affect the music to which they were set. A similar influence came from the Lutheran chorales, which used simple metrical patterns so that the congregation could keep together. As a result of these and kindred influences, western music steadily lost the plasticity of rhythm it had had during the Middle Ages and the Renaissance.

The movement toward standardized metrical rhythm reached its height in the Classic-Romantic era. Indeed, practically the entire output of the eighteenth and nineteenth centuries—an enormous amount of music—was written in two-four, three-four, four-four, and six-eight time—that is, two, three, four, or six beats to a measure, with a regularly recurring accent on the first beat. . . .

Musicians found the excessive standardization of meter increasingly hostile to artistic expression, and sought to free themselves from the trip-hammer obviousness of the accented beat.

167

These attempts began long before the twentieth century. Older masters, for instance, made liberal use of *syncopation,* a technique of shifting the accent to the off-beat, thereby upsetting—and enlivening—the normal pattern of accentuation. Composers also used more complex subsidiary rhythms within the measure. A characteristic subtlety was *cross rhythm:* shifting the accents within the measure so that a passage written in triple time briefly took on the character of duple time, or the other way around. Much favored too was the simultaneous use of two rhythmic patterns, such as "two against three" or "three against four." These devices figure prominently in the music of Chopin, Schumann, and Brahms.

A great impetus towards the freshening of rhythm came from the nationalist schools of the nineteenth century. Rhythms drawn from Polish, Hungarian, Bohemian, and Norwegian folk dance enlivened the standard patterns of the older musical cultures. The Russians played a leading role in this development. Musorgsky especially used rugged, uneven rhythms of great expressive power. In the final quarter of the century it became ever clearer that new conceptions of rhythm were in the making.

The revolt against the standard meters led twentieth-century composers to explore the possibilities of less symmetrical patterns. At the same time poets were turning from metrical to free verse. Both these developments reflect a general tendency in contemporary art to pull away from conventional symmetry in favor of the unexpected. As one critic expressed it, "We enjoy the irregular more than the regular when we understand it."

The revitalization of western rhythm was nourished by a number of sources. Composers felt obliged to try to capture the hectic rhythms of the life about them. Nineteenth-century rhythms were derived from peasant dances and bucolic scenes. Twentieth-century rhythms glorify the drive of modern city life, the pulsebeat of factory and machine. It is therefore natural for twentieth-century musicians to be preoccupied with that element of their art most closely associated with movement and physical activity. Also, the enormous popularity of Russian ballet in the years after the First World War heightened the emphasis on rhythm. Nineteenth-century composers had concentrated on harmony and orchestral color, and had somewhat neglected rhythm. The New Music had to correct the imbalance.

In their desire to escape the obvious, composers began to draw inspiration from rhythmic conceptions outside European music. Especially fruitful was the interest in primitive art that arose in the opening years of the century. The pounding, hammering rhythms of Stravinsky and Bartók sent a breath of fresh air through European music. Not unrelated were the syncopations of jazz that became the rage in Europe and exerted a positive influence on contemporary music. The search for new rhythmic effects led composers far afield in time as well as space. They turned back to the free prose rhythms of Gregorian chant; they studied the supple rhythms of medieval motet and Renaissance madrigal, in which no single strong beat regularized the free interplay of the voices. Nationalism, too, made a vital contribution to the new rhythm. Vaughan Williams in England, Bartók in Hungary, and Charles Ives in the United States prized the rhythms of their cultures precisely for their "off-beat" qualities. From the interaction of all these forces came a new rhythm, tense and resilient, that electrified the world.

The twentieth-century composer is apt to avoid four-bar rhythm. He regards it as too predictable, hence unadventurous. He prefers to challenge the ear with nonsymmetrical rhythms that keep the listener on his toes. This rejection of standard patterns has led composers to explore meters based on odd numbers: five beats to the measure $(3 + 2$ or $2 + 3)$; seven $(2 + 2 + 3, 4 + 3,$ or $2 + 3 + 2)$; nine $(5 + 4,$ or $4 + 5)$; also rhythms based on groups of eleven or thirteen beats. Within the measure small units of beats are subdivided in a great diversity of rhythmic patterns. In addition, the grouping of the bars into phrases is far more flexible than in earlier music. The result is that today rhythm is freer, more supple than ever before.

Often, in nineteenth-century music, an entire piece or movement is written in a single meter. Twentieth-century composers, striving for the suppleness of free-verse and prose rhythm, began to change from one meter to another with unprecedented rapidity and ease. In a word, they turned to *multirhythm*. . . .

This continual change of time generates an excitement that is most congenial to the modern temper. In a multirhythmic passage such as the one above, the unit of meter is no longer the measure—how can it be if it is changing constantly?—but the single beat. This becomes the nucleus of small rhythmic motives which combine in larger groups to produce an incisive, self-generating rhythm. The new motor rhythm is thus liberated from the bonds of conventional meter, to become a powerful expressive agent, a constructive force that keeps the sonorous material in a state of dynamic impulsion. . . .

Occidental musicians marvel at the intricate patterns set up by African drummers who execute conflicting rhythms simultaneously. Similar effects abound in the music of the percussion orchestras of the far east. Contemporary composers have captured something of this intricacy, using conflicting rhythmic patterns that unfold at the same time: in a word, *polyrhythm*. . . .

Another device characteristic of contemporary rhythm is the *ostinato* (literally, "obstinate," that is, recurring over and over). Precedents for this device abound in the music of the seventeenth and early eighteenth centuries, in which a phrase in the bass would be repeated again and again (called *basso ostinato*) while above it the upper voices traced a set of variations. Twentieth-century musicians have adopted this procedure, basing the ostinato not on a melodic phrase but on a persistent rhythmic pattern. The ostinato is unsurpassed as a means of building up excitement. However, like all striking effects it must be used with caution as it easily degenerates into mannerism.

Twentieth-century rhythm, like melody and harmony, has abandoned the landmarks on which the mass of music lovers depend. In much contemporary music (although by no means all!) the listener will miss the reassuring downbeat, the predictable accent that is so pleasant to nod, tap, and sway to, just as he will miss the symmetrical phrase-and-cadence structure based on four-bar rhythm. As he accustoms himself to do without those, he will discover a world of fresh and novel rhythms, impregnated with kinetic power and movement, and thoroughly tuned to the modern world. The emancipation of rhythm from the standard metrical patterns of the eighteenth and nineteenth centuries must be accounted one of the major achievements of the New Music. It has resulted in nothing less than a revitalization of the rhythmic sense of the West. . . .

Texture

The nineteenth century completed the swing from a horizontal to a vertical conception of music. Texture throughout the Romantic era emphasized harmony and color rather than line. Composers were preoccupied above all with unlocking the magic power of the chord. This striving for luscious harmony impelled them to an ever richer orchestral sound. Texture grew thick and opaque. The mammoth orchestra favored by the disciples of Wagner—Richard Strauss, Mahler, and the youthful Schoenberg—brought the overelaborate textures of the post-Romantic era to a point beyond which no further progress was possible.

There is a healthy impulse in art to execute an about-face when an impasse has been reached. Contemporary music found a new direction.

In pulling away from the emotional exuberance of the post-Romantic era, composers turned also against the sumptuous texture that was its ultimate manifestation. They had to lighten the texture, they felt, in order to give music once again a sense of unobstructed movement. The twentieth century thus saw a great revival of counterpoint, which represented a return to the esthetic ideals of the age of Bach, the last period when the horizontal-linear point of view had prevailed. Composers broke up the thick chordal fabric of the late Romantic style; they shifted from opulent tone mass to pure line, from sensuous harmony and iridescent color to sinewy melody and transparency of texture. The "return to Bach" extended beyond the work of that master to the great contrapuntists of the fifteenth and sixteenth centuries. This new interest in linear thinking served the desire of the age for condensation of style and purity of expression, for athletic movement and architectonic unity; above all, for a point of view that concentrated upon compositional problems rather than upon the expression of personal feelings.

The interest in counterpoint did not exclude the lively exploration of new harmonic resources that we traced in an earlier chapter. The two currents flowed side by side, each nourishing the other. We saw that the "skyscraper" chords of contemporary music are really polychords which create several planes of harmony—what we referred to as polyharmony. Composers now began to employ polyharmony in the service of the new counterpoint, and combined independent successions of chords just as their predecessors used to combine single lines of melody. It was as if each melodic strand of the old counterpoint had been thickened out to become a composite stream of harmony. In such music the contrapuntal interplay is no longer between lines of single notes, but between moving blocks of harmony which are heard on separate planes. The several streams of sound may approach one another or separate, clash or coalesce, exactly as did the individual parts in the older polyphony. The resulting sound is wholly of the twentieth century. . . .

It should be added that polyrhythms also served the cause of the new linear texture. They reinforced the independence of the lines, contributing materially to achieving the contrast and inner tension which are the life blood of counterpoint

Consonance unites, dissonance separates. The masters of polyphony in the past used consonant intervals—fifths, fourths, thirds, and sixths—at the decisive points of contact between the voices, so as to blend them into a unified texture. Contemporary composers, on the other hand, try to make the several lines stand out from one another. They use dissonances (seconds, sevenths, augmented and diminished intervals) to clarify the vertical sound and the disposition of the voices.

This purposeful kind of texture is known as *linear counterpoint*. The term is redundant, as all counterpoint is based on line and linear thinking. The adjective, however, emphasizes the fact that each line of this texture aspires to independence without trying to combine with the other voices. In recent years the more descriptive term *dissonant counterpoint* has come to denote the kind of texture in which dissonance energizes the movement and adds to the propulsive power of the lines.

The reconstitution of contrapuntal values must be regarded as one of the prime achievements of twentieth-century music. It has revealed to composers anew the expressive powers of melody and the constructive values of line. It has also restored the balance that was upset by nineteenth-century emphasis upon vertical elements at the expense of horizontal. Contemporary music has instituted counterpoint not as an accessory technique but as an integral part of the compositional process. As the English critic George Dyson put it, "Ours is an age of texture." . . .

Orchestration

The orchestra of Haydn and Mozart was capable of subtle nuances by which each timbre was made to stand out luminously. The eighteenth-century masters used their medium with surpassing economy. Color, for them, did not exist as an end in itself. It sprang from the nature of the thing said; it served the idea. Color highlighted form and structure, and contributed to achieving architectural unity.

For the Romantic composers, color was an end in itself, and a perpetual source of wonder. Richard Strauss well understood this when he remarked that Hector Berlioz "was the first composer consistently to derive his inspiration from the nature of the instruments." In this regard the pioneering Frenchman was a true romantic. Until his time, as Aaron Copland pointed out, "composers used instruments in order to make them sound like themselves; the mixing of colors so as to produce a new result was his achievement."

It was Richard Wagner who created the sound image of the Romantic orchestra which is most familiar to the world. His habit of blending and mixing colors continually, his technique of reinforcing (doubling) a single melody line with various instruments, and his addiction to sustained tones in the brass produced a rich massive texture that enchanted the audiences of the late nineteenth century. His was an opulent, multicolored cloud of sound in which the pure timbres of the individual instruments were either veiled or completely swallowed up; hence the frequent remark that Wagner's orchestra plays "with the pedal on." This technique was carried to its farthermost limits in the post-Romantic era, culminating in the orchestral virtuosity of Richard Strauss. Orchestration became an art that existed almost independently of composition. The composer displayed his sense of sound with the same mastery that former composers had shown in the field of thematic invention. The post-Romantic period saw the emergence of other brilliant orchestrators besides Strauss—Gustav Mahler, Maurice Ravel, Ottorino Respighi. But it happened in more than one work that the magnificence of the orchestral raiment far surpassed the quality of the musical ideas.

Between 1890 and 1910 the orchestra assumed formidable proportions. Strauss, in his score for *Elektra,* called for twelve trumpets, four trombones, eight horns, six to eight kettledrums. In Mahler's *Symphony of a Thousand* several choruses were deployed, in addition to mammoth orchestral forces. The texture of music began to assume a complexity beyond the capacity of the human ear to unravel. Despite the furious interplay of the instrumental lines, what emerged was a swollen, opaque stream of sound that brought to its ultimate development the vertical-harmonic—that is to say, the sheerly romantic—way of hearing music. The post-Wagnerian orchestra reached a point beyond which further advance was hardly possible.

Such an orchestral style, needless to say, could not appeal to a generation of musicians in revolt against the romantic esthetic. Debussy speaks of the "thick polychromatic putty" that Wagner spread over his scores. Stravinsky remarks that Wagner's orchestra "plays the organ." Copland describes the German master's orchestration as "an over-all neutral fatness of sound which has lost all differentiation and distinction." This change of taste went hand-in-hand with the simplification of texture described in the last chapter, and brought with it a lightening of the orchestral sound. Twentieth-century composers forced the post-Romantic orchestra to open its window, so to speak: to let in light and air.

175

The turn from harmonic-vertical to contrapuntal thinking determined the new orchestral style. The nineteenth-century musician made his colors swim together; his twentieth-century counterpart aspires above all to make each instrument stand out clearly against the mass. Composers have turned back to classical ideals: clarity of line and transparency of texture. They have thinned out the swollen sound and reinstated the sharply defined colors of the eighteenth-century style. They no longer reinforce or double the melody line with a blend of instruments from various choirs; instead they emphasize individual timbres. As Stravinsky put it, "Doubling is not strengthening."

One may compare this change to a rejection of the rich composite colors of oil painting in favor of the naked lines of etching. The new orchestration reveals the interweaving of the melodic strands, the play of contrapuntal lines rather than the flow of harmonic masses. The result has been a reconstruction of true orchestral polyphony. There has been a return to the classical precept that color must function not as a source of enchantment but as a means of clarifying the structural design. The leaders of contemporary musical thought have emphasized again and again the need to free music from the seduction of Romantic sonority. "We must outgrow the sentimental and superficial attachment to sound," wrote Paul Hindemith. Arnold Schoenberg maintained that "Lucidity is the first purpose of color in music. Perhaps the art of orchestration has become too popular, and interesting-sounding pieces are often produced for no better reason than that which dictates the making of typewriters and fountain pens in different colors." Stravinsky also warns against the "fundamental error" of regarding orchestration as "a source of enjoyment independent of the music. The time has surely come to put things in their proper place."

The desire to "decongest" the Romantic sound brought in its wake a strong desire for a reduction of orchestral forces. From the monster ensemble of the 1890s, composers turned back to the smaller orchestra of the early nineteenth century. They revived the chamber orchestra of the eighteenth century—an ensemble of about twenty men in which each player functioned almost as a soloist. The adherents of the new classicism aspired to the radiant clarity of Mozart's orchestral texture, and to the *concertante* style of the age of Bach, in which single players or small groups opposed each other by their timbres instead of blending into a composite work. . . .

At the same time contemporary musicians continued the nineteenth century attempt to open up new orchestral resources, using instruments in unusual ways, and exploring the expressive power of extreme registers and novel combinations. They exploited new effects—for example, the trombone glissando that Schoenberg employed so imaginatively. It can safely be said that musicians today are more adept in the art of orchestration than ever before. What with the prevalence of good orchestras, recordings, and radio, they have greater opportunities than did musicians of any earlier generation to hear orchestral music well played. As a result, many a young composer nowadays sets forth on his career with a mastery of orchestral technique it would have taken him half a lifetime to acquire a century ago.

Twentieth century music is extremely dependent upon the orchestral medium. We are able to get some idea of a Classic or Romantic symphony from a piano transcription; but this is hardly possible with modern works. Often a dissonance which sounds painfully harsh when a contemporary score is played on a piano has a luminous glow when it is heard in its proper spacing and timbre in the orchestra.

The advances in orchestral technique achieved during the nineteenth century made possible a new orchestral art. In restoring orchestral color to its function in classical times as the obedient handmaiden of form and idea, twentieth-century composers found a way to make the orchestra serve the esthetic goals of our time. . . .

Form

Considering the great changes that have taken place with respect to melody, harmony, rhythm, color, texture, and tonality, the changes in musical form have been considerably less spectacular. The traditional forms offer such ingenious solutions to the problem of unity and variety in music that they are not easily supplanted. The most important trend has been a moving away from the clear-cut symmetries of the Classic-Romantic era. The phrase is still the unit of musical architecture; but its beginning and end are no longer punched home to the ear. Repetition remains the basic principle of musical structure—but repetition disguised, varied, cropping up at irregular intervals and unexpected places. The whole conception of form based on clearly articulated formations of two, four, and eight measures has been drastically modified. This veiling of the structural outlines has resulted, naturally, in a certain loss of clarity and simplicity. But it has brought a corresponding gain of subtlety and freshness in expressive resources. "It is the barely perceptible irregularities that infuse life into artistic form," writes Ernst Toch. Contemporary music has rediscovered the charm of the irregular. . . .

Our time avoids grandiloquence and verbosity, and rejects the over-extended forms of the post-Wagner period. The twentieth-century climate is hospitable to epigrammatic statement, to forms that are forthright and laconic. The emphasis is on nicety of detail, precision of thought, and simplicity of means.

At the beginning of our century the sonata form had apparently been rendered obsolete. It was overwhelmed on the one hand by Wagnerian music drama and the Straussian tone poem, on the other by the pictorial creations of Debussy and Ravel. The revival of classical canons of taste has restored the absolute forms to a central position in our musical life.

The Classical sonata embodied the structural values inseparable from the major-minor system: contrasting key centers, clearcut harmonic cadences, sharply defined phrase structure, symmetrical sections, vertical texture, and the ultimate resolution of the Dominant harmony to the Tonic. But these are precisely the values that have either been abandoned or severely modified in the contemporary style. That the sonata has been able to accommodate itself to so changed an environment testifies to the extraordinary vitality of the grand form.

Contemporary harmony has expanded the sense of key; it is therefore evident that all musical forms based on tonality have had to be modified. We will not find in the modern sonata, whether for piano, string quartet or orchestra, the old Tonic-Dominant relationship, or a clearly molded bridge passage between the home key and the contrasting key. Transitional passages—the seams of musical fabric—are not favored today. Modulations are swift and abrupt, dispensing with the traditional connectives: one tonality is simply displaced by another. Key relationships, as might be expected, are extremely flexible and free. All the same, tonality still plays an important part in stabilizing harmonic areas and tonal masses. . . .

The themes of the modern sonata are apt to be instrumental in character rather than vocal (as was the case during the Romantic period). They are relatively short, precise, impregnated with movement and gesture, with motoric rhythm and propulsive force. They are building blocks in the fullest sense, lending themselves readily to developmental procedures and to contrapuntal combination. The distinction in style between Exposition and Development is observed far less today than in the Classic-Romantic era. Indeed, the modern sonata movement has largely given up the neatly sewn, three-section fabric of the

Classical pattern. Development has taken over the entire form, pervading Exposition and Restatement as well. As a result, the modern sonata form tends to be one continuous development from first note to last, a procedure that accords with the dynamic concept of form of our time. Often a movement unfolds without a full cadence from beginning to end, relinquishing clarity of punctuation in favor of uninterrupted momentum. More themes may be presented, and with less regularity than in the Classical sonata. Connective passages may introduce new ideas that are immediately subjected to development. The arch of the form extends in a single span, with an unfaltering drive that steadily mounts in tension.

Equally significant are the changes in the cycle as a whole. Twentieth-century esthetics has come to grips with what was always a vulnerable spot in the sonata cycle. We all know that if we come too late to hear the first movement of a symphony, concerto, sonata, or string quartet, as like as not we have missed the most important part of the work. In many a work of the Classic-Romantic era the later movements hardly match the tension of the first. Contemporary musicians have tried to avoid the inevitable sense of anticlimax in one of three ways. First, by placing the most dramatic and spacious movement at the end of the cycle rather than at the beginning. (The late works of Beethoven already utilize this solution of the problem.) Second, by amalgamating the four movements into a single-movement form with contrasting sections; this retains the diversity of the classical cycle in condensed fashion. (The precedent here was established by Liszt.) Third, by reshuffling and interlocking the movements. The component sections of one movement are often lifted out of their context and linked with parts of another movement. In one sonata we may find a slow section interposed between Exposition and Development, while a scherzo-like section intervenes between Development and Restatement. In another, Exposition and

Restatement may be separated to become the first and last parts of the cycle, providing a flexible frame for the intervening movements. The possibilities are manifold, and have been exploited very imaginatively by contemporary musicians.

It should be added, however, that present-day composers do not feel impelled to abandon the traditional scheme unless their expressive purpose demands it. The serious artist does not court innovation for its own sake. . . .

The twentieth-century concept of form derives from the great tradition. Composers have taken from the old forms whatever could be of use to them, and have added new elements, thereby adapting the achievements of the past to the needs of the present. In our time, as formerly, they affirm the primacy of form in the musical tradition of the west: form as the supreme gesture of ceative will and imagination; as the subjugation of all that is capricious and arbitrary to the discipline, the logic, the higher unity of art.

24

Roger Sessions

1896-

PROBLEMS AND ISSUES FACING THE
COMPOSER TODAY

Roger Sessions is an American composer and teacher, at
Princeton University, who has often written about the con-
temporary musical scene. Among his writings is: *The Musical
Experience of Composer, Performer, Listener*. The present ar-
ticle originated in a special seminar on "Problems of Modern
Music," held at Princeton University in the summer of 1959.

THE HISTORY OF Western music reveals at least two phases, and
possibly three, that may well have seemed to those who observed
them as contemporaries to shake the art of music to its depths
and to raise questions of the most fundamental kind—questions,
that is, not only as to the character and trend of current developments, but as to the function, the significance, and even the ultimate nature of music itself. They were periods of apparent
crisis, during which long-established values were brought into
deep question and challenged both on the most profound and
the most superficial levels; "experimental" periods in the sense
that many things were tried which soon proved abortive, while
others, soon discarded, seemed to find justification at a much
later date; but periods of intense creativity not only by virtue
of the music of genius that survived them, but because they

182

tapped new veins, uncovering the resources out of which the music of the following three or four centuries was to be built. In each period the musical transformation was coeval with a far-reaching transformation in Western society, and undoubtedly related to it, though the exact nature of this relationship seems—at least to this writer—far more difficult to penetrate and to clarify than it is frequently assumed to be.

The period in which we live has at the very least much in common with these earlier ones. For well over a hundred years each successive generation has seemed to many of its members to contain within itself the seeds of the imminent destruction, not only of a great musical tradition, but possibly of music itself. Though this had happened at earlier periods also, it has happened at a steadily increasing tempo since, roughly, the death of Beethoven. Each generation has, to be sure, at length become assimilated, by and large, to the "main stream"; the "revolutions" have in each case been discovered eventually to be not so revolutionary after all, and the revolutionaries of one generation have become symbols of conservatism and eventually clubs with which to beat their revolutionary successors of the next. But, with each succeeding phase, this has come about a little more slowly, and there is no doubt an easily discernible reason for this. It is true that in our time the situation of all the arts, and in all of their phases, has been rendered far more complex, first through the development of mass media, and the consequent immeasurable expansion of the more-or-less interested public, and secondly through various economic factors, including not only the decline of private patronage and the consequent and inevitable increase in commercialization, but drastically rising costs in virtually every phase of musical production. It is however no less true that, precisely at this moment of economic and, if you will, social crisis in the arts, the inner dynamic of music itself should be leading to developments of which the eventual result can at best be only dimly sensed.

One symptom—or result—of this, of course, may be seen in the increasing articulateness of musicians themselves in regard to their own artistic principles. Since the early years of the 19th century composers have felt more and more inclined to express themselves in print regarding music and all of its phases. In the case of earlier composers—Mozart and Beethoven, for instance—one must rely on correspondence, on reminiscences, and on a few sybilline and perhaps problematic quotations that have become traditional, and no doubt often distorted, if one wants to discover their working principles beyond the evidence of the music itself. From [the early 19th century] on, however, composers have devoted considerable effort and energy to criticism, later to theory, and more recently still to teaching. This is certainly due in very large part to the fact that, in a period of artistic upheaval, creative artists find themselves first of all sharply aware of their own relationship to their traditional inheritance and to the directions in which they feel impelled to extend or even to reject it. Secondly, they find themselves, in a period in which the formulated notions regarding musical esthetics, musical theory, and musical syntax have long since lost the vitality they once possessed, impelled or even obliged to arrive at what are at least working formulations of their own.[1] If they are not to remain in relative solitude they are also likely to communicate these formulations. Since the cultural pessimism of our time abhors solitude—once considered a decidedly honorable state for an artist—and demands "news" at almost any price, they may even find themselves virtually compelled to do so.

One has only to open practically any European periodical devoted to living music in order to become aware of the intellectual ferment that characterizes the musical life of today. One will find there, as one finds in fact on all hands, serious and often acute discussion of every phase, from generalized esthetic attitudes to the most precise and esoteric matters, and on a level

[1] See also Stravinsky's statements on these points.—*Ed.*

that the conscientious artist of mature age, or the ambitious one of more tender years, cannot wholly ignore except at the price of an inherent lack of adventurousness which in itself bodes somewhat ill for his achievement as an artist. I of course do not mean to imply by this that he is bound to accept all or even any of the ideas he will find urged upon him. But he will find himself, certainly, challenged at every point, and obliged to find his own answer to the challenges thus presented to him; and if he is young and gifted he will welcome these challenges as a test of his creative conviction, if not as a source of direct stimulation along the lines of his own expression. At the very least, he will have the opportunity to become more aware of his own musical nature, and at the best he will learn to be untiring in his effort to avail himself of that opportunity, and to pursue his own creative efforts accordingly.

That the situation as I have described it contains its own peculiar pitfalls is, of course, obvious. One cannot insist too strongly or too frequently that, in the arts generally and in music in particular, it is only productions that really count, and that only in these—music, written or performed—are to be found the criteria by which ideas about music, as well as music itself, must finally stand or fall: not the converse.

The generic pitfall at which I have hinted is precisely this one. In an age in which theoretical speculation in either the esthetic or the technical sphere has assumed the importance it has in our own, there is always the danger that it may be overvalued, and assumed to furnish criteria in itself, and not regarded simply as a means that may prove useful in helping composers to achieve the artistic results they are seeking—in the realization, that is, of a genuine musical vision. Again, one finds oneself obliged to emphasize that the primary function of the composer is to possess, develop, and with the utmost intensity to realize his own particular vision—a vision which, if it is genuinely vital, will be found to contain both general and

185

specifically personal elements; and that theory and esthetics can have validity for him only in so far as they can find roots in this vision. Otherwise they can represent only a flight away from music, or at a very dubious best, a crutch on which a faltering musical impulse can find some measure of support.

It is in fact fairly easy to recognize the pitfalls characteristic of those past musical periods with which we are most familiar. To a certian extent they are mirrored in the way in which these periods are regarded by the succeeding generations, which rebel against them. The characteristic pitfall of the 19th century was undoubtedly that of literary association and the manner of over-emphasis—sentimental, violent, or pretentious—just as that of the 18th was a certain type of elegant and formal convention-ality. Our own particular brand of emptiness is perhaps begin-ning to emerge in a variety of clichés, derived both from so-called neo-Classicism[2] and from serialism[3] in its earlier as well as its later phases. In each case we are dealing with a manner that has become generalized through lack of substance, and not with ideas in any positive sense. What is necessary, if the pitfalls are to be avoided, is that composers in the first place should al-ways retain the courage of their own artistic vision, that teachers should emphasize the supremacy of real musical imagination, and that listeners, of whatever category, should, by holding themselves open to whatever genuine and even unexpected ex-perience music can bring, learn to discriminate between what is authentic and what is fictitious.

Thus far I have spoken at length of a general situation in the musical world, and of some of the questions that situation raises as such, without attempting to deal with the situation itself, its

[2] A movement prevalent in the 1920s in which composers incorporated features of the music of the 18th century and earlier in their works.—*Ed.*

[3] A way of composing often associated with Arnold Schoenberg and his followers. It is based on maintaining a succession of musical materials, as chosen by the composer for that piece, throughout the composition, un-altered except according to a few basic rules. The materials most frequently arranged in this manner are the twelve pitches, but durations, volume, and other materials may be similarly arranged.—*Ed.*

background, or its nature, other than to characterize it in the very generalized sense of the decay of one tradition and the gradual movement towards new factors capable of superseding it. The ultimate shape these developments will assume is still by no means definitive in its outlines; but both their causes and their present trends are in certain respects quite clear, as are the specific questions posed by the latter.

It seems clear, for example, that the development of harmony as we have traditionally conceived it has probably reached a dead end. First of all, composers have for many years felt able to utilize all possible vertical combinations of tones, and have so abundantly availed themselves of that possibility that any new discoveries in this regard are virtually unthinkable. Even this fact, however, tells only a part of the story, since the possibilities are not so rich as this purely statistical assumption would indicate. As more and more tones are added to any chord, each added tone contributes less to the character of the chord, or, in other words, to the factor that differentiates it from other combinations of tones. The decisive development of harmony, therefore, depends overwhelmingly on combinations of a relatively small number of tones; beyond that number, so to speak, the ear refuses to interest itself in strictly harmonic effect. It is not so much a question of possibilities as such, as of possibilities that are in any way decisive. The real point is that composers seem by and large no longer interested in chords as such, and that this is a tacit recognition that there is nothing left to be discovered, in the sphere of harmony, that arouses any feeling of excitement on their part.

Something similar had of course taken place already in regard to functional harmony. Based very clearly on a triadic premise, the principle of root progression had given way before the proliferation of "altered chords" that was so characteristic a feature of harmonic evolution in the 19th century. What is often called "atonality" was a very gradual development—so gradual, in fact, that, aside from the literal meaning of the term itself, it is impossible to define with any precision whatever. It is in other words impossible to show exactly where tonality ends and "atonality" begins unless one establish wholly arbitrary lines of demarcation in advance.

This is not the main objection to the term, however. "Atonality" implies music in which not only is the element of what is defined as "tonality" no longer a principle of construction, but in which the composer deliberately avoids all procedures capable of evoking "tonal" associations. Actually this is virtually impossible, owing to the mere fact that we use tones, and hear them in relation to each other. In other words, whenever a series of tones is heard, the musical ear assimilates it by perceiving a pattern composed not only of tones but of intervals; and neither the process nor the sensation is different in any essential principle from the process by which one assimilates music that is unimpeachably "tonal."

If the cadence, as conventionally defined, came finally to seem to many composers, in the context of their own music, little more than a cliché, it was because they came to feel a definite disparity between the harmonic vocabulary native to them and the harmonies necessary to establish the cadence. While the composers of the late 19th century—one senses the problem already in the music of Wagner—succeeded in overcoming this disparity, often through sheer technical ingenuity and sometimes with visible effort, their successors often found this impossible to achieve without stylistic violence. It was necessary either to turn backward or to seek new principles.

A similar development took place in the rhythmic sphere. It took place more quietly and with far less opposition, if indeed there was any appreciable opposition whatever. There is no need to dwell on the rhythmic question here. Though the changes that have taken place have been equally far-reaching, they have been in a sense less spectacular and less esoteric, if only for the reason that they owe so much to the influence of popular music and of early chant. They have found incomparably more ready acceptance, both from musicians and from the general public, than the developments of which I have spoken in the realm of harmony. Furthermore, the rhythmic aspects of music are bound closely and inevitably to the other elements of the musical vocabulary; in this sense one can say that the development of music away from the tonal and cadential principle has also created a whole new set of rhythmic premises and requirements.

In any event, the focal point of the more advanced musical thought of today is polyphonic, and more concerned with problems of texture and organization than with harmony in the hitherto accepted meaning of the term. Once more, this does not mean that composers have ceased to be acutely aware of vertical relationships between tones, of progressions from one vertical conglomerate to another, or even of the patterns formed by such progressions. But it is certainly true, I think, that they tend more and more to think of these matters in terms of texture rather than harmony as hitherto defined. The current trend is to refer to such vertical conglomerates as "densities" rather than as "chords" or "harmonies"; but it must be stressed that there is no satisfactory substitute for awareness of the entire musical context, and that the replacement of one term by another is useful in so far as it increases that awareness, and does not connote the evasion of one issue in favor of another.

This brings us to the large question of serialism, which I have deliberately postponed till after discussing some of the factors that have given rise to it. One cannot, of course, stress too much that serialism is neither the arbitrary nor the rigid set of prescriptions that it is often supposed to be, not only by its foes but unfortunately also by some of its friends. It is rather the result of many converging trends of musical development, of which I have mentioned a couple of the most important and the most general ones. Above all, perhaps, it is the result of the decreasing validity of the harmonic principle as an organizing force, and the necessity of adopting consistent relationships between tones, which can serve as a constructive basis for the organization of musical ideas, along both the horizontal and the vertical dimensions.

Quite as important is to stress that serialism is in full process of development, and that the shapes it has taken are already manifold. It is a technical principle that a wide number and variety of composers have found useful for their own purposes, both because of the organizing principles they have derived from it and because of the musical resources it has opened up for them. Like any other technical principle, it yields nothing in itself; it is always for the imagination of the composer to discover what it can give him, and to mold it to his own uses. Its value lies wholly in the music of the composers who have seen fit to adopt it, and the value of that music resides in the imaginative, emotive, and constructive force inherent in it, not in the ingenuities with which the system is applied, except in so far as these are the inherent result of a musical conception.

The serial organization of tones must be, and for the most part is, today regarded as a settled fact—the composer is free to take it or leave it, or to adopt it with varying degress of rigor, as he may choose. The results it can yield are open to all to see and judge as they see fit. More problematical are some attempts that have been made to extend serial organization to other aspects of music—notably to that of rhythmic values and that of dynamics. Any discussion of these matters must emphasize once more that it is only results that matter; that the human imagination works along channels that are frequently unexpected, and that a critical scrutiny of technical premises does not release one in the slightest degree from the responsibility of holding one's mind, ear, and heart open to whatever may reveal genuinely new vistas of musical expression and experience.

With this caution in mind one can easily observe that tones

are, for the musical ear, fixed and readily identifiable points in musical space, and that the progress from one tone to another has a clear point of departure and arrival. This is partly the result of the fact that within the octave there are only twelve tones, with which the musical ear has familiarized itself over the course of many centuries; and the additional fact that our musical culture has taught us to regard as equivalent tones that occupy the same position within the various octaves. A, for instance, is recognizable as A whether it be played on the open A string of the double bass, of the 'cello, or of the violin—or, for that matter, in the high register of the flute or the piccolo. Time values, on the other hand, are by no means fixed; their range is to all intents and purposes infinite. This does not at all exclude the possibility of adopting an arbitrary series of time values for the purposes of any single composition, but it does raise very valid questions regarding the serialization of time values as a general principle. The serialization of dynamics, however, raises questions of a much more fundamental nature. Dynamic values are by their very essence relative, both in an objective and a subjective sense. They have quite different meanings for different media and under different conditons. How can we regard as equivalent, except on the most practical level of balance, a given nuance on, say, the oboe and the violin, or for that matter, the same nuance in different registers of the same instrument; or on the same note on the same instrument, sounded in a small room, a large concert hall, and the open air? What does the indication *piano* actually mean, and how can we as listeners distinguish in clear terms a transition from *mezzoforte* to *forte*, or even from *mezzopiano* to *fortissimo*?

The subject of "total organization" leads naturally to the consideration of electronic media, since the latter make possible the exact control of all musical elements, and make possible in a sense also a partial answer to some of the questions I have raised. Since the potentialities of electronic media in the realm of sound are, at least to all intents and purposes, infinite, it is possible to measure all musical elements in terms of exact quantity, and in fact necessary to do so, since such measurement is the very nature of the instruments and the method by which they are used. A dynamic nuance thus not only can, but must, become a fixed quantity, as can and must, also, any tone in the whole range of pitch or color gradations. Every moment of music not only can but must be the result of the minutest calculation, and tthe composer for the first time has the whole world of sound at his disposal.

That electronic media will play a vital and possibly even decisive role in the future of music is not to be doubted. I must confess however to skepticism as to what that precise role will be. Two questions seem to me to be crucial. First of all, it is not sufficient to have the whole world at one's disposal—the very infinitude of possibilities cancels out possibilities, as it were, until limitations are discovered. No doubt the limitations are there, and if not there they are certainly in human beings. But the musical media we know thus far derive their whole character and their usefulness as musical media precisely from their limitations—stringed instruments derive their character and utility from not only the fact that they are stringed instruments, that the tone is produced by stroking strings, but from the fact that they are not wind or percussion instruments; and we have learned to use them with great subtlety of effect and power of expression because of that. The dilemma of electronic musical media is a little like that of the psychologist who is reputed once to have said to one of his friends, "Well I have got my boy to the point where I can condition him for anything I want. What shall I condition him for?"

The other question has to do with the essential nature of music itself. Is music simply a matter of tones and rhythmic patterns, or in the final analysis the organization of time in terms of human gesture and movement? The final question regarding all music that is mechanically reproduced seems to be bound up with the fact that our active sense of time is dependent in large degree on our sense of movement, and that mechanical repetition mitigates and finally destroys this sense of movement in any given instance; it destroys also our sense of expression through movement, which plays so large and obvious a part in our musical experience. This is what lies behind the discussions of the element of "chance," which has so bothered the proponents of "total organization." But the element that "total organization" leaves out of account is not chance at all. It is the organic nature of movement as such, of the fresh and autonomous energy with which the performer invests each musical phrase, every time he sings or plays it, and which gradually disappears for our awareness if we listen so often to a mechanical reproduction of it that we become completely familiar with it, to the point of knowing always exactly what is coming next. It is more than the element of mere "surprise"; it is rather that if the expression of movement is to become effective, we require not only the evidence of movement from one point to the next, but a sense of the motivating energy behind it.

To raise these questions is not in any sense to reject the principle of electronic music as such. In the first place, composers are beginning to feel the need for new instruments. The existing ones, for all their technical perfection, are beginning at times to seem vaguely obsolete as far as some of the composers' musical ideas are concerned. The possibilities electronic music suggests are altogether likely to make this situation more acute.

In my own opinion, electronic media more than justify their existence if only by the new insight one can gain from them into the nature of sound, musical and otherwise, and above all by a vast quantity of fresh experience they can provide, on the purely acoustical level. They are still in a clearly very primitive stage and it is impossible to say what they may contribute in the future. But they raise the above questions and many others, and the questions will certainly become more acute as the media develop.

One hears a good deal, these days, of the developing "dehumanization" of music and the other arts; and specifically in regard to the tendencies we discussed in detail at the Princeton Seminar last year, and which I have been discussing in these pages. This is all very well, and not without its plausibility; but we are speaking of a movement that is widespread among the younger composers of Europe, that has begun to take root in the United States, and that above all is in constant development and evolution. Many ideas are being tested, and many are quickly discarded. If we regard certain manifestations with raised eyebrows, that is our privilege as members of an older generation, as it is always our privilege to point out flaws in logic. But if it is also our prerogative to insist on the primacy of the creative imagination, and to minimize the decisive importance of theoretical speculation, we are at the same time obliged to abide by our own premises, and look towards artistic results rather than towards the ideas by which these are rationalized. By the same token it is well to remember that art, considered on the most objective level, reflects the attitudes of the individuals that produce it. The danger of dehumanization is a real and patent one, and the individual can, and certainly should, resist any dehumanizing tendency with all his strength. But this cannot, and must not, blind us to the claims of whatever is genuinely new and vital in the arts, or, once more, cause us to forget that it is the product, not the process, that is of real importance; and that the creative imagination, at its most vital, has revealed himself through many and often surprising channels. There is no reason to believe that it will not continue to do so, as long as creative vitality—which for musicians means above all the intense love of music—continues to persist.

25

Igor Stravinsky

1882-

THE COMPOSITION OF MUSIC

The composer, Igor Stravinsky, gave a series of lectures at Harvard University (1939-1940) which were later published as *Poetics of Music in the Form of Six Lessons*. The present excerpt is from the third lesson.

IT IS THROUGH the unhampered play of its functions . . . that a work is revealed and justified. We are free to accept or reject this play, but no one has the right to question the fact of its existence. To judge, dispute, and criticize the principle of speculative volition which is at the origin of all creation is thus manifestly useless. In the pure state, music is free speculation. Artists of all epochs have unceasingly testified to this concept. For myself, I see no reason for not trying to do as they did. I myself having been created, I cannot help having the desire to create. What sets this desire in motion, and what can I do to make it productive?

The study of the creative process is an extremely delicate one. In truth, it is impossible to observe the inner workings of this process from the outside. It is futile to try to follow its successive phases in someone else's work. It is likewise very difficult to observe one's self. Yet it is only by enlisting the aid of introspection that I may have any chance at all of guiding you in this essentially fluctuating matter.

Most music-lovers believe that what sets the composer's creative imagination in motion is a certain emotive disturbance generally designated by the name of *inspiration*.

I have no thought of denying to inspiration the outstanding role that has devolved upon it in the generative process we are studying; I simply maintain that inspiration is in no way a prescribed condition of the creative act, but rather a chronologically secondary manifestation.

Inspiration, art, artist—so many words, hazy at least, that keeps us from seeing clearly in a field where everything is balance and calculation through which the breath of the speculative spirit blows. It is afterwards, and only afterwards, that the emotive disturbance which is at the root of inspiration may arise—an emotive disturbance about which people talk so indelicately by conferring upon it a meaning that is shocking to us and that compromises the term itself. Is it not clear that this emotion is merely a reaction on the part of the creator grappling with that unknown entity which is still only the object of his creating and which is to become a work of art? Step by step, link by link, it will be granted him to discover the work. It is this chain of discoveries, as well as each individual discovery, that gives rise to the emotion—an almost physiological reflex, like that of the appetite causing a flow of saliva—this emotion which invariably follows closely the phases of the creative process.

All creation presupposes at its origin a sort of appetite that is brought on by the foretaste of discovery. This foretaste of the creative act accompanies the intuitive grasp of an unknown entity already possessed but not yet intelligible, an entity that will not take definite shape except by the action of a constantly vigilant technique.

This appetite that is aroused in me at the mere thought of putting in order musical elements that have attracted my attention is not at all a fortuitous thing like inspiration, but as habitual and periodic, if not as constant, as a natural need.

This premonition of an obligation, this foretaste of a pleasure, this conditioned reflex, as a modern physiologist would say, shows clearly that the idea of discovery and hard work is what attracts me.

The very act of putting my work on paper, of, as we say, kneading the dough, is for me inseparable from the pleasure of creation. So far as I am concerned, I cannot separate the spiritual effort from the psychological and physical effort; they confront me on the same level and do not present a hierarchy.

The word *artist* which, as it is most generally understood today, bestows on its bearer the highest intellectual prestige, the privilege of being accepted as a pure mind— this pretentious term is in my view entirely incompatible with the role of the *homo faber.*[1]

At this point it should be remembered that, whatever field of endeavor has fallen to our lot, if it is true that we are *intellectuals,* we are called upon not to cogitate, but to perform.

The philosopher Jacques Maritain reminds us that in the mighty structure of medieval civilization, the artist held only the rank of an artisan. "And his individualism was forbidden any sort of anarchic development, because a natural social discipline imposed certain limitative conditions upon him from without." It was the Renaissance that invented the artist, distinguished him from the artisan and began to exalt the former at the expense of the latter.

At the outset the name artist was given only to the Masters of Arts: philosophers, alchemists, magicians; but painters, sculptors, musicians, and poets had the right to be qualified only as artisans.

> Plying divers implements
> The subtile artizan implants
> Life in marble, copper, bronze,

[1] I.e. "Man making things."—*Ed.*

says the poet Du Bellay. And Montaigne enumerates in his *Essays* the "painters, poets and other artizans." And even in the seventeenth century, La Fontaine hails a painter with the name of *artisan* and draws a sharp rebuke from an ill-tempered critic who might have been the ancestor of most of our present-day critics.

The idea of work to be done is for me so closely bound up with the idea of the arranging of materials and of the pleasure that the actual doing of the work affords us that, should the impossible happen and my work suddenly be given to me in a perfectly completed form, I should be embarrassed and nonplused by it, as by a hoax.

We have a duty toward music, namely, to invent it. I recall once during the war when I was crossing the French border a gendarme asked me what my profession was. I told him quite naturally that I was an inventor of music. The gendarme, then verifying my passport, asked me why I was listed as a composer. I told him that the expression "inventor of music" seemed to me to fit my profession more exactly than the term applied to me in the documents authorizing me to cross borders.

Invention presupposes imagination but should not be confused with it. For the act of invention implies the necessity of a lucky find and of achieving full realization of this find. What we imagine does not necessarily take on a concrete form and may remain in a state of virtuality, whereas invention is not conceivable apart from actual working-out.

Thus, what concerns us here is not imagination in itself, but rather creative imagination: the faculty that helps us to pass from the level of conception to the level of realization.

In the course of my labors I suddenly stumble upon something unexpected. This unexpected element strikes me. I make a note of it. At the proper time I put it to profitable use. This gift of chance must not be confused with that capriciousness of imagination commonly called fancy. Fancy implies a predetermined will to abandon one's self to caprice. The afore-mentioned assistance of the unexpected is something quite different. It is a collaboration immanently bound up with the inertia of the creative process and is heavy with possibilities which are unsolicited and come most appositely to temper the inevitable over-rigorousness of the naked will. And it is good that this is so.

"In everything that yields gracefully," G. K. Chesterton says somewhere, "there must be resistance. Bows are beautiful when they bend only because they seek to remain rigid. Rigidity that slightly yields, like Justice swayed by Pity, is all the beauty of earth. Everything seeks to grow straight, and happily, nothing succeeds in so growing. Try to grow straight and life will bend you."

The faculty of creating is never given to us all by itself. It always goes hand in hand with the gift of observation. And the true creator may be recognized by his ability always to find about him, in the commonest and humblest thing, items worthy of note. He does not have to concern himself with a beautiful landscape; he does not need to surround himself with rare and precious objects. He does not have to put forth in search of discoveries: they are always within his reach. He will have only to cast a glance about him. Familiar things, things that are everywhere, attract his attention. The least accident holds his interest and guides his operations. If his finger slips, he will notice it; on occasion, he may draw profit from something unforeseen that a momentary lapse reveals to him. . . .

The faculty of observation and of making something out of what is observed belongs only to the person who at least possesses, in his particular field of endeavor, an acquired culture and an innate taste. A dealer, an art-lover who is the first to buy the canvases of an unknown painter who will be famous twenty-five years later under the name of Cézanne—doesn't such a person give us a clear example of this innate taste? What else guides him in his choice? A flair, an instinct from which this taste proceeds, a completely spontaneous faculty anterior to reflection.

As for culture, it is a sort of upbringing which, in the social sphere, confers polish upon education, sustains and rounds out academic instruction. This upbringing is just as important in the sphere of taste, and is essential to the creator who must ceaselessly refine his taste or run the risk of losing his perspicacity. Our mind, as well as our body, requires continual exercise. It atrophies if we do not cultivate it.

It is culture that brings out the full value of taste and gives it a chance to prove its worth simply by its application. The artist imposes a culture upon himself and ends by imposing it upon others. That is how tradition becomes established.

Tradition is entirely different from habit, even from an excellent habit, for habit is by definition an unconscious acquisition and tends to become mechanical, whereas tradition results from a conscious and deliberate acceptance. A real tradition is not the relic of a past irretrievably gone; it is a living force that animates and informs the present. In this sense the paradox which banteringly maintains that everything which is not tradition is plagiarism, is true . . .

Far from implying the repetition of what has been, tradition presupposes the reality of what endures. It appears as an heirloom, a heritage that one receives on condition of making it bear fruit before passing it on to one's descendants.

Brahms was born sixty years after Beethoven. From the one to the other, and from every aspect, the distance is great; they do not dress the same way, but Brahms follows the tradition of Beethoven without borrowing one of his habiliments. For the borrowing of a method had nothing to do with observing a tradition. "A method is replaced: a tradition is carried forward in order to produce something new." Tradition thus assures the continuity of creation. The example that I have just cited does not constitute an exception, but is one proof out of a hundred of a constant law. This sense of tradition which is a natural need must not be confused with the desire which the composer feels to affirm the kinship he finds across the centuries with some master of the past.

My opera *Mavra* was born of a natural sympathy for the body of melodic tendencies, for the vocal style and conventional language which I came to admire more and more in the old Russo-Italian opera. This sympathy guided me quite naturally along the path of a tradition that seemed to be lost at the moment when the attention of musical circles was turned entirely toward the music drama, which represented no tradition at all from the historical point of view and which fulfilled no necessity at all from the musical point of view. The vogue of the music drama had a pathological origin . . .

The music of *Mavra* stays within the tradition of Glinka and Dargomizhsky. I had not the slightest intention of reestablishing this tradition. I simply wanted in my turn to try my hand at the living form of the *opéra-bouffe* which was so well suited to the Pushkin tale which gave me my subject. *Mavra* is dedicated to the memory of composers, not one of whom, I am sure, would have recognized as valid such a manifestation of the tradition they created, because of the novelty of the language my music speaks one hundred years after its models flourished. But I wanted to renew the style of these dialogues-in-music whose voices had been reviled and drowned out by the clang and clatter of the music drama. So a hundred years had to pass before the freshness of the Russo-Italian tradition could again be appreciated, a tradition that continued to live apart from the main stream of the present, and in which circulated a salubrious air, well adapted to delivering us from the miasmic vapors of the music drama, the inflated arrogance of which could not cancel its vacuity.

I am not without motive in provoking a quarrel with the

notorious Synthesis of the Arts. I do not merely condemn it for its lack of tradition, its *nouveau riche* smugness. What makes its case much worse is the fact that the application of its theories has inflicted a terrible blow upon music itself. In every period of spiritual anarchy wherein man, having lost his feeling and taste for ontology, takes fright at himself and at his destiny, there always appears one of these gnosticisms which serve as a religion for those who no longer have a religion, just as in periods of international crises an army of soothsayers, fakirs, and clairvoyants monopolizes journalistic publicity. We can speak of these things all the more freely in view of the fact that the halcyon days of Wagnerism are past and that the distance which separates us from them permits us to set matters straight again. Sound minds, moreover, never believed in the paradise of the Synthesis of the Arts and have always recognized its enchantments at their true worth.

I have said that I never saw any necessity for music to adopt such a dramatic system. I shall add something more: I hold that this system, far from having raised the level of musical culture, has never ceased to undermine it and finally to debase it in the most paradoxical fashion. In the past one went to the opera for the diversion offered by facile musical works. Later on one returned to it in order to yawn at dramas in which music, arbitrarily paralyzed by constraints foreign to its own laws, could not help tiring out the most attentive audience in spite of the great talent displayed by Wagner.

So, from music shamelessly considered as a purely sensual delight, we passed without transition to the murky inanities of the Art-Religion, with its heroic hardware, its arsenal of warrior-mysticism, and its vocabulary seasoned with an adulterated religiosity. So that as soon as music ceased to be scorned, it was only to find itself smothered under literary flowers. It succeeded in getting a hearing from the cultured public thanks only to a misunderstanding which tended to turn drama into a hodgepodge of symbols, music itself into an object of philosophical speculation. That is how the speculative spirit came to lose its course and how it came to betray music while ostensibly trying to serve it the better. . . .

Let us understand each other in regard to . . . fantasy. We are not using the word in the sense in which it is connected with a definite musical form, but in the acceptation which presupposes an abandonment of one's self to the caprices of imagination. And this presupposes that the composer's will is voluntarily paralyzed. For imagination is not only the mother of caprice, but the servant and handmaiden of the creative will as well.

The creator's function is to sift the elements he receives from her, for human activity must impose limits upon itself. The more art is controlled, limited, worked over, the more it is free.

As for myself, I experience a sort of terror when, at the moment of setting to work and finding myself before the infinitude of possibilities that present themselves, I have the feeling that everything is permissible to me. If everything is permissible to me, the best and the worst; if nothing offers me any resistance, then any effort is inconceivable, and I cannot use anything as a basis, and consequently every undertaking becomes futile.

Will I then have to lose myself in this abyss of freedom? To what shall I cling in order to escape the dizziness that seizes me before the virtuality of this infinitude? However, I shall not succumb. I shall overcome my terror and shall be reassured by the thought that I have the seven notes of the scale and its chromatic intervals at my disposal, that strong and weak accents are within my reach, and that in all of these I possess solid and concrete elements which offer me a field of experience just as vast as the upsetting and dizzy infinitude that had just frightened me. It is into this field that I shall sink my roots, fully convinced that combinations which have at their disposal twelve sounds in each octave and all possible rhythmic varieties promise me riches that all the activity of human genius will never exhaust.

What delivers me from the anguish into which an unrestricted freedom plunges me is the fact that I am always able to turn immediately to the concrete things that are here in question. I have no use for a theoretical freedom. Let me have something finite, definite—matter that can lend itself to my operation only insofar as it is commensurate with my possibilities. And such matter presents itself to me together with its limitations. I must in turn impose mine upon it. So here we are, whether we like it or not, in the realm of necessity. And yet which of us has ever heard talk of art as other than a realm of freedom? This sort of heresy is uniformly widespread because it is imagined that art is outside the bounds of ordinary activity. Well, in art as in everything else, one can build only upon a resisting foundation: whatever constantly gives way to pressure constantly renders movement impossible.

My freedom thus consists in my moving about within the narrow frame that I have assigned myself for each one of my undertakings.

I shall go even farther: my freedom will be so much the greater and more meaningful the more narrowly I limit my field of action and the more I surround myself with obstacles. Whatever diminishes constraint diminishes strength. The more constraints one imposes, the more one frees one's self of the chains that shackle the spirit.

To the voice that commands me to create I first respond with fright; then I reassure myself by taking up as weapons those things participating in creation but as yet outside of it; and the arbitrariness of the constraint serves only to obtain precision of execution.

From all this we shall conclude the necessity of dogmatizing on pain of missing our goal. If these words annoy us and seem harsh, we can abstain from pronouncing them. For all that, they nonetheless contain the secret of salvation: "It is evident," writes Baudelaire, "that rhetorics and prosodies are not arbitrarily invented tyrannies, but a collection of rules demanded by the very organization of the spiritual being, and never have prosodies and rhetorics kept originality from fully manifesting itself. The contrary, that is to say, that they have aided the flowering of originality, would be infinitely more true."

26

Arnold Schoenberg

1874-1951

ON DISSONANCE AND MODERN MUSIC

Arnold Schoenberg is identified with the twelve-tone, or
serial, technique of musical composition. The extract included
here is from an article entitled *Problems of Harmony* (1934).

TONALITY DOES NOT DEPEND on the number of dissonances used,
nor on their eccentric effect, but rather

(1) on whether these chords may be referred to a key; or
(2) whether these relations are convincingly enough worked
out.

Dissonances, even the simplest, are more difficult to comprehend than consonances. And therefore the battle about them
goes on throughout the length of music history. The number of
consonant chords is limited; in fact, it is rather small. The
number of dissonances is so great that it would be difficult to
systematize the relation of even the simplest ones to all the
consonances and to each other, and to retain them in memory.
With the majority of dissonances the ear meets a new and
unknown situation, often a situation for which there is not the
slightest analogy. How difficult it was even with the four and
five-tone dissonant chords for the hearer not to lose the sense of
coherence! But as soon as the ear grew accustomed to such
sounds and tonal combinations, recognizing old acquaintances,
it learned also not to lose the coherence, even though the

solution of the problem was revealed not immediately but later.

It is easier to recognize and define three different, simultaneously sounding tones than five or six; it is easier to follow and to perceive the succession of three, than of five or six. But is the use of polyphonic chords therefore unjustified because they are more difficult to apprehend?

The criterion for the acceptance or rejection of dissonances is not that of their beauty, but rather only their perceptibility. The recognition of coherence, logic, conclusiveness is one of the most important conditions for the apprehension of what occurs, and one can only understand what one has retained in memory. If *a* plus *b* equals *c*, I can conceive *c* in the sense of *a* plus *b* only if I remember *a* and *b*; only thus can I sum them up as equal to *c*. Since the presence of complicated dissonances does not necessarily endanger tonality, and since on the other hand their absence does not guarantee it, we can ask now, what are the characteristics of that music which is today called "atonal." Permit me to point out that I regard the expression atonal as meaningless, and shall quote from what I have already expounded in detail in my treatise on Harmony. "Atonal can only signify something that does not correspond to the nature of tone." And further: "A piece of music will necessarily always be tonal in so far as a relation exists from tone to tone, whereby tones, placed next to or above one another, result in a perceptible succession. The tonality might then be neither felt nor possible of proof, these relations might be obscure and difficult to comprehend, yes, even incomprehensible. But to call any relation of tones atonal is as little justified as to designate a relation of colors aspectral or acomplementary. Such an antithesis does not exist."

I am usually not a coward; but if I should be asked to give this phenomenon a name, I would prefer—to avoid it entirely. But a habit has arisen of regarding music first, not with the ears by listening, second, not with the eyes by playing and reading it, and third, not with the mind but according to some technical peculiarity, for which there is a suitable slogan, a most striking term. "This symphony is impressionistic!" Yes, but has something occurred to the writer? "This song is expressionistic!" Yes, but does the composer know anything? "This piano piece is atonal!" Yes, but does it contain an idea? And how is it accomplished? And what does the composer say that is new? or worth while saying?

If audiences and musicians would ask about these more important things and attempt to receive answers by listening, if further they would leave the idle talk and strife rather to the school-masters, who also must have something to do and wish to make a living, I, who have the hope that in a few decades audiences will recognize the *tonality* of this music today called *atonal,* would not then be compelled to attempt to point out any other differences than a *gradual* one between the tonality of yesterday and the tonality of today. Indeed, tonal is perhaps nothing else than what is understood *today* and atonal what will be understood in the *future.* In my *Harmony* treatise I have recommended that we give the term "pantonal" to what is called atonal. By this we can signify: the relation of all tones to one another, regardless of occasional occurrences, assured by the circumstance of a common origin.

I believe, to be sure, that this interrelationship of all tones exists not only because of their derivation from the first thirteen overtones of the three fundamental tones, as I have shown, but that, should this proof be inadequate, it would be possible to find another. For it is indisputable that we can join twelve tones with one another and this can only follow from the already existing relations between the twelve tones.

Now let us briefly recapitulate the assertions already advanced. Tonality has been revealed as no postulate of natural conditions, but as the utilization of natural possibilities; it is a product of art, a product of the technique of art. Since tonality is no condition imposed by nature, it is meaningless to insist on preserving it because of natural law. Whether, for artistic reasons, tonality must be retained depends on whether it can be replaced. Since, as I have pointed out, the logical and artful construction of a piece of music is also secured by other means, and since the lack of tonality only increases the difficulty but does not exclude the possibility of comprehension; and since further proof of lack of tonality has not yet been adduced but as, on the contrary, probably much that today is not regarded as tonal, may soon be so accepted; and since dissonances need not in the least disturb tonality, no matter how increasingly difficult they may make the understanding of a work; and inasmuch as the use of exclusively tonal chords does not guarantee a tonal result, I come to the following conclusion: music which today is called "tonal" establishes a key relationship continuously or does so at least at the proper moment; but music which is today called "not tonal" never allows predominance of key relationships. The difference between the two methods is largely in the emphasis or non-emphasis on the tonality. We further conclude that the manner of composition of a piece abandoning tonality in the traditional sense must be different from that in which tonality is followed. From this angle tonality is seen as *one of the means* which facilitates the unifying comprehension of a thought and satisfies the feeling for form. But since this means alone does not achieve the goal, it may be said that tonality accomplishes but a part of the purpose. If the function of tonality be dispensed with, but the same consideration be given to unity and feeling of form, this effect must be achieved by some other function. Obviously music so contrived can hardly be easy to grasp at the present time.

To prove the correctness of an idea no special method of

order and construction in its presentation is demanded. The effort of the composer is solely for the purpose of making the idea comprehensible to the listener. For the latter's sake the artist must divide the whole into its parts, into surveyable parts, and then add them together again into a complete whole now conceivable in spite of hampering details. Experience teaches us that the understanding of the listener is an unstable quantity: it is not permanently fixed. Fortunately! It gradually accommodates itself to the demands made on it by the development of art. How otherwise would it have been possible, in scarcely more than sixty years, to follow the leaps and bounds of musical development that have led us from Wagner through Mahler, Reger, Strauss and Debussy to the harmony of today? Many are still living who can recall the difficulties presented to their sense-perception by the dissonances of Wagner. Certainly there must still be many today who only a short time ago found Mahler, Strauss, Reger and Debussy incomprehensible; yet today these composers must appear to them, at least in their manner of expression, self-evident. No longer does one lose the thread in their compositions—insofar as one holds it at all—because of incomprehensible harmonic passages. Nothing now hinders the understanding of their thoughts, the recognition of their melodies, of the flow and construction of their works. What at first appeared harmonically incoherent, wild, confused, arbitrary, eccentric and hideous is today felt to be beautiful.

If we imagine that the perceptive faculties of audiences will advance nearly as far in the near future as in those past years, then we must have faith that we shall achieve a true knowledge of the ideas presented today and an understanding of their beauty. The difficulty here is, in the first instance, to recognize and to feel in the polyphonic dissonant sounds, the capacity to be joined successively; to see in them elements of form and construction in the same manner as in the simple chords, and to feel also their relative measure of weight and significance just as in the older harmonies. Theoretical knowledge here is not the most essential need. Wagnerian and post-Wagnerian music was understood for a number of years before the derivation of certain chords and their relation to the key were theoretically established. Probably habit is all that is required; for it is able to prevent the recurrence of shock and the resultant lapse of presence of mind. He who is frightened is seldom in a position to follow exactly what is happening. Should such a one be accepted as witness, or rather one who does not lose presence of mind and remains calm, is enraptured or stirred only through the power of the idea and the emotion?

Index